Hunting Dogs from Around the World

In collaboration with Suzel Vervaet

Graphical Conception and Realization Bleu T

See pages 223 and 224 for Contents

Consulting Editor: Matthew M. Vriends, Ph.D.

All of the photographs were taken by Dominique and Serge Simon, with the exception of those on pages 78, 79, 181, and 189, which were taken by Jean-Michel Lepeudry.

All inquiries should be addressed to:
Barron's Educational Series, Inc.
250 Wireless Boulevard
Hauppauge, NY 11788

Library of Congress Catalog Card No. 97-12172

International Standard Book No. 0-8120-6632-4

Library of Congress Cataloging-in-Publication Data
Lepeudry, Jean-Michel.
  [Chiens de chasse. English]
  Hunting dogs / Jean-Michel Lepeudry, Dominique and Serge Simon.
          p.   cm.
    Includes bibliographical references and index.
    ISBN 0-8120-6632-4
    1. Hunting dogs. 2. Hunting dogs—Pictorial works. I. Simon, Dominique. II. Simon, Serge. III. Title.
  SF428.5.L4613   1997
  636.75—dc21   97-12172
                                                       CIP

Printed in Hong Kong

987654321

Jean-Michel Lepeudry

Dominique and Serge Simon

Hunting Dogs from Around the World

BARRON'S

Summary

Preface

For the hunter, the hunting dog is not an accessory on the same level as his shotgun or his boots. For him the hunting dog often represents a very large part of the pleasure of hunting. The dog is truly at the very heart of hunting, and many are the hunters who have said "Without my dog, I would not hunt!" However, this indispensable companion has undergone and continues to undergo many evolutions.

Purebred dogs are gaining more and more ground compared to those of mixed breed. Today's hunter is more demanding. In many parts of the country small game is becoming scarcer because the countryside has been radically altered by a veritable revolution in agriculture. All of that has given way to immense plains. Agricultural chemicals are omnipresent. Small game owes its survival in many places to the efforts of hunters. Moreover, not only are small game animals less numerous, but they have also become more distrustful by a hostile environment that allows them to spot danger from a good 330 feet (100 meters) away. Consequently, the hunter who does not own a very effective dog has little chance of bagging big or small game.

Migratory birds, especially woodcocks, are more "educated" and therefore more difficult to approach. All these factors demand from dogs a higher level of performance, ardor, enterprise, and efficiency. Without a doubt, hunters from the 1930s would be surprised to see the remarkable dogs that we have today, considering that back then, even very average dogs were used to hunt game.

But hunters expect not only performance; they also want beauty in the art of hunting. Today, hunting is no longer seen in terms of quantity but also in terms of quality. This means that the enjoyment of hunting no longer comes from capturing game, but rather from the way this capturing is accomplished with the dog's help. This beauty of hunting is not gratuitous; it is the style inherent in each breed. This style is very important because it reveals all the characteristics that make a breed perfectly adapted to the kind of hunting for which it was conceived. Thus a pointer is beautiful while galloping with its head high and not bent toward the ground. This position is the dog's own style of hunting, but it is also the best way for a

pointer to smell game from large distances, since the scent of a sitting bird spreads widely through the air. If it were not in this position the pointer that gallops very quickly would not smell the game until it was already upon it—that is, too late. Taken by surprise, the dog would be unable to stop the bird from flying away. Dog lovers use the term, "striking" the bird, to describe such a dog performance. The beauty with which a pointer carries its head is thus proof of its perfect effectiveness. Certainly, this principle holds true for every breed.

The more difficult the hunt, the better hunting dogs perform and the more fascinating they are to watch. But the public is totally unaware of the hunting dog's evolution. Popular imagery always depicts the rural hunter walking on a plowed field at dawn with his dog leaping around him. This image, even though a caricature, nevertheless symbolizes the importance of the relationship between the hunter and his dog. Paradoxically, the latest studies on the subject show that for many reasons people have a better opinion of hunters with dogs than without. First of all, the love for dogs is one of the characteristics of our society, and a man who loves his dog, as a hunter does, cannot look altogether unlikable even to people who are upset by the idea of hunting itself. It is as if the dog brings together hunters and nonhunters. Another good reason is that hunting dogs, unlike other breeds, are unanimously recognized as being among the nicest breeds. Even if this popular belief is questionable, it has some basis in reality: hunting dogs today are among the only dogs able to expend their energy and even aggressiveness in a healthy way when they hunt, which undoubtedly makes them very well adjusted. Consequently, unlike hunting, hunting dogs are accepted by most people. One might be a ferocious opponent of hunting but it is difficult to be ferociously opposed to hunting dogs—even though they hunt!

Hunting dogs hunt. This truism contains an extremely important element that hunters have no doubt been unable to take advantage of until now. Hunting dogs chase game, point it, catch it, and retrieve it—all without any guilt. Better still, the dog is made for this very purpose and nobody sees anything shocking in this. One would not dispute the right of the sheepdog to look after sheep, any more than the right of a Brittany to catch partridges, simply because, to the Brittany, hunting is a natural thing to do. The word is out. For dogs, hunting is a normal activity—that goes without saying. Consequently, why deny humans—predatory animals themselves from time immemorial—this same right?

In the wilderness, dogs, like any other predator, do not behave as compulsive carnivores. Dogs hunt to feed themselves and kill only what they need for subsistence without endangering future generations of their prey. Today our pet dogs do not need to hunt in order to eat. Neither do we. At any rate, the instinct to hunt is so strong and the enjoyment so intense, that dogs continue to hunt, just as we do. Similarly, it is up to us, predators endowed with reason, to do everything we can to keep hunting from threatening our prey—wild game—with extinction. Without prey there would be no predators; without game, no dogs or hunters.

Following pages: The critical, emotional moment: a pack of small Blue Gasconies set upon a hare.

A hunting dog is first of all a daily companion, whatever the breed. One must learn how to live with the dog and how to integrate it into the "pack" to which it will ultimately belong: the human family. There are two ways to do this: either humans consider the dog as one of them and attribute human feelings and behavior to it or, aware of the differences between man and dog, the members of the human family seek first to understand the dog's reactions before knowing how to behave toward it. The first option is the most frequently encountered, and the second, the only one likely to create good living conditions for both parties. The intention of the first part of this book is to give very practical, simple, and clever advice drawn from actual experience.

Choosing a Hunting Dog

Choosing Rationally and Not Sentimentally

Following page, above: Hunting with a pointer (here, a German Shorthaired Pointer hunting young partridge in the Beauce region near Chartres) is demanding. Indeed, the hunter must be able to hunt alone over relatively vast areas.

Bottom: The courageous Beagle, the hound that many hunters prefer, is, at the same time, a compact, biddable, and very versatile dog.

The hunter does not choose a dog as someone looking for a pet would. The hunting dog is a precious helper that is supposed to fulfill a well-defined function that is indispensable to the success of his master's passion. As a result, choosing a dog depends upon specific criteria that are obviously not the same as those for choosing a house dog.

Hunters often make the mistake of choosing a breed according to characteristics that have nothing to do with rational judgment. Choosing a hunting dog must be first and foremost the result of long-term reflection. It is essential to ask oneself a certain number of questions. The first one is obvious: "Which dog is the one best adjusted to the types of hunting that I practice?" Thus, it is not yet a question of choosing the right breed but simply the right "type" of dog.

Two big categories exist: dogs intended to hunt small game and those intended to hunt big game.

If the hunter is especially fond of large animals, he will be drawn to four types of dogs. Medium-sized or big hounds are used especially in packs. They permit one to hunt deer and wild boar on horseback or with a rifle over vast areas. Because of their great speed, these dogs are not suitable in small areas whose limits they would quickly overrun in pursuing game. Small hounds are used

under the same conditions but in smaller areas because their slower speed permits them to be stopped before they overrun the limits of the areas they cover. The same advantage exists with terriers, although their drawback is a weaker bark (music to the hunter's ears), but they have more of a bite and better discipline.

The last category is bloodhounds, which appeal equally to stalking hunters who do not need a helper to track game, as well as to battue hunters, who wish to enlist the aid of a helper to complement their main pack of dogs.

For the hunter of small game, the problem is more difficult because the choice is wider. The pointer appeals especially to those who hunt alone or in small groups over a relatively large area. If the hunter practices his sport in a group over smaller distances, he must choose a spaniel instead. He may also opt for a retriever if he hunts most frequently from a blind or if he hunts waterfowl. Finally, the small game hunter who encounters mostly rabbits should choose small hounds like bassets. The hare hunter might also use one or several hounds, but of a larger breed.

The important thing is not to choose a hunting dog too impulsively. Hunters of young partridges would have no use for a retriever or a small hound, just as duck hunters would be bothered by a galloping

dog like the pointer. A breed may look attractive, but if it is not entirely suitable to the kind of hunting practiced, the hunter risks compromising his hunting pleasure for the next ten years to come. Thus, rather than fawn all over a little ball of fur in a store window, it is better to take ample time to consider the choice calmly. This is the best way for the hunter to have an excellent hunting dog at his disposal in the future.

CHOOSING RATIONALLY AND NOT SENTIMENTALLY

Choosing a Breed

The Pointer is very suitable for the solitary hunter in an open field, but can also adapt to many other environments.

Once the type of dog has been well defined, which seems relatively simple, the choice of an actual breed remains. Here, things get much more complicated. If the hunter decides in favor of a pointer, why would he choose the English Setter rather than the Gordon Setter? Why the German Shorthaired Pointer rather than the Weimaraner?

Many hunters base their choice on esthetic criteria, favoring the coat of one breed over that of another. Some begin an attempt to think it over, which is also often a mistake: "My friend X owns a breed of dog that is extraordinary with young partridges; so this breed should be right for me since I hunt pheasants." Finally, it is true that certain breeds are amazing or fashionable or unusual. Therefore, they might represent a sign of social status for the hunter that will impair his judgment.

In fact, there is always one breed that is perfectly adapted to each hunter. This breed is not always the one of which he would have thought. The high number of existing breeds (about seventy main breeds) is not merely a result of an aesthetic desire for variety. Each breed was created for a definite use. Each dog corresponds to a particular hunting situation to which dog breeders of the past knew how to provide a perfectly suitable answer. It is rare to see a dog of a certain breed perform a given task with the same effectiveness as another breed.

Therefore, it is useless to flip through the pages of dog books like a mail-order catalog. In fact, only one or two breeds will perfectly suit any given hunter. Of course, this does not mean that the other breeds cannot perform the same task. They can do so, but always with less effectiveness and, when all is said and done, they give less pleasure to the hunter. Consequently, it is better to own a dog that is not exactly the one the hunter was dreaming about, but one that fulfills its role thus bringing its master maximum satisfaction when hunting.

In order to answer the difficult question of which breed to choose, the hunter must have one indispensable item: a mirror. Indeed, the hunter will find a satisfactory answer to his needs by carefully observing himself. This is particularly true of the hunter of small game who should first consider his physical condition.

Certain breeds of pointers are very fast. This is the case for English breeds, such as Setters and Pointers, but also for some others, such as the modern Brittany (p. 97) and the German and French hounds of today. These dogs hunt fast and far and are made for locating hares and difficult game in wide-open spaces. They need a master in good shape, who

will be able to follow them in this very active search. It is pointless to choose them if the hunter is rather old or if intense physical exertion is not part of the pleasures that the hunter looks for in hunting.

For the less physical hunter, it is best to choose a less impetuous and more diligent breed such as the American Water Spaniel, the Basset Hound, the Deerhound, or the Wirehaired Pointing Griffon.

Choosing a breed also depends on a second criterion: the hunting territory where the hunter practices his sport. If the territory is small and the number of fellow hunters significant, it is best to forget about pointers. This is especially the case with relatively bushy territory. As a matter of fact, the pointer is not suited to this kind of hunting either, because this dog needs space and time to work effectively. The competition among a great number of dogs and the discipline of walking

This Blue Belton English Setter (with a black-and-white coat) is equally at ease in plains, swamps, and in the woods.

Brittanies are known mostly for their orange and white coat. However, many other varieties exist, such as the black-and-white one shown in this photo.

happen to be the solution. These dogs hunt "under the gun" and therefore do not disturb the other participants. Real "raking machines," they never miss any game, from rabbits to pheasants, including migratory birds. Endowed with perfect retrieving and great obedience, spaniels are the ideal for hunting in bushy areas. Springers are rather quick dogs and cockers are hard-working; there are dogs to suit all tastes.

In group hunting, several hunters often take up their positions at equal distances. In this situation, the hunter does not need a dog capable of finding living game, but rather a helper whose retrieving is perfect.

There are also many areas where ducks regularly pass by at the end of the hunting day. In both situations, retrievers are the most suitable dogs. They stay obediently at their master's feet, leaving to retrieve dead or wounded game only upon his order. Nothing can make these dogs abandon their search until they find the coveted animal.

The retriever is often the ideal dog for group hunting where dogs that can flush four-footed game abound, yet where each day, some game is lost because of the lack of dogs specialized in retrieval.

Hunters of furry game, from rabbits to wild boars, who must use hounds, will choose the dog breed according to the particular terrain in which they hunt. Certain breeds are more apt to manage in very enclosed areas where thorn bushes proliferate. Others bear the torments of the sun and the heat better, while still other breeds show themselves particularly fit for tackling difficult terrain. This book should help those who want to find the most appropriate hunting dog for the types of hunting they engage in.

necessary for a line of ten hunters do not allow the pointer to develop a quartering of 55 yards (50 meters) on each side of his master. Nor will the hunter be able to pass in front of two or three persons in order to see exactly where his dog is pointing. Finally, another dog will invariably interfere with the pointer's concentration. Therefore, it is necessary to consider choosing a different type of dog for group hunting in small areas and spaniels just

Pedigree or Mutt?

In various European and Asian countries, dogs without registration papers and even those of no identifiable breed have a very good reputation with a large number of hunters. Born of haphazard and doubtful crossbreeding on a remote farm, or of the desire of a man to crossbreed his good dog with his neighbor's dog, mongrels, or mutts, are numerous because only a low percentage of those dogs have a pedigree. The percentage, in France, for example (only 10%), is considerably less than in Great Britain or in Germany where purebred dogs represent about 50% of the canine stock. Are mongrels truly better hunting dogs than purebred dogs? It is appropriate at this point to clear up a few misconceptions.

Purebred dogs are not more mentally or physically fragile than dogs without pedigree. Dog breeders practice a rigorous selection. They systematically remove dogs with anomalous traits from the breeding process. This misconception of purebred dogs might come from the fact that a purebred is more expensive. The owner thus takes more precautions for the animal and very quickly discovers any anomalous traits his dog might have. On the other hand, the defects of a mongrel of obscure origins are more likely to escape notice. Less is expected of

Purebred dogs

Every purebred dog is entitled to a pedigree, and it is presented to you when you pick up the puppy at the breeder's home. In this document are recorded not only the name and origin of the dog, but those of its parents and grandparents as well, along with any show titles won. The AKC registration certificate confirms that the puppy is purebred, with its dam and sire both being registered dogs.

"I knew a grandfather who hunted with an exceptional mongrel! This dog was able to flush any kind of game, from thrushes to wild boars— there was no lost game. A dog of extraordinary intelligence, this mongrel had nothing in common with those completely degenerate purebreeds." What hunter has never heard such remarks?

One must not confuse
a crossbreed with a
mutt. The former is a
dog born of two
purebred dogs of
different pedigrees,
while the latter is the
fruit of two dogs of
no identifiable breed,
although even the
lowly mutt, like a
crossbreed, ultimately
descends from
pedigrees.

a mongrel, whereas the dog with a pedigree must show proof of its noble origins.

Nor are mongrels better hunters than pedigrees. Indeed, exceptions exist and any given crossbred dog might appear particularly brilliant, but it is risky to make this a general rule based on a few isolated cases. Purebreds prove their effectiveness during very strict training competitions from which only the best emerge victorious. It is these select dogs that are used for breeding. Mongrels are renowned only through the hearsay of their owners, through whose subjective eyes their dog is always the best. No reliable process of selection exists for mongrels. By contrast, selecting dogs for

over a century according to their performance can only improve a breed. Finally, we should never forget that mongrels are perhaps considered good dogs precisely because they are born of purebred dogs.

When the hunter chooses a mongrel, he takes a big risk because he has no guarantee concerning the puppy's actual abilities. A pleasant surprise is possible, but too often people forget that the great majority of these dogs are worthless for hunting. Therefore, there is a considerable risk of ending up with a really mediocre dog.

Choosing a purebred dog requires a more rational approach. The future purchaser must first get information concerning the results achieved by breeders and more generally, must inquire about the whole breeding process. This certainly does not mean that he will find the perfect dog. However, choosing a dog from a breeder known for results in field events represents a sure guarantee for the purchaser of the performance of his future companion. Therefore, one should not hesitate to resort to such reputable breeders.

Adopting a dog from the Humane Society is certainly laudable, but this does not necessarily guarantee good results in the field.

A Puppy or a Mature Dog?

Once the prospective dog buyer has decided to acquire a purebred dog and selected the desired breed, he must then choose between a puppy and a full-grown dog that has already been trained. Actually, this question arises only in the case of dogs intended for small-game hunting. Indeed, hounds and terriers are rarely sold when they are full-grown, except for breeding purposes or to put them in existing packs.

For pointers, but also for retrievers and spaniels, the sale of full-grown already trained dogs is becoming more and more widespread. But for all that, the two-and-a-half-month-old puppy is not neglected. Each approach has its advantages.

Right now, purchasing a puppy from a breeder is the most widespread method of buying a dog. Generally, the young dog is given to the hunter when it is eight to ten weeks old, when it is developmentally in what is known as the "human socialization period." This period, which lasts only until the puppy is about twelve weeks old, is the best time for a dog to learn to live with humans.

It is recommended that a puppy be separated from its dam and littermates and placed in the home during the eighth week of life because this is when permanent bonds are formed. If allowed to remain with the litter, the primary bond will be to dogs rather than to humans, which hinders the human-dog relationship. In other words, the only thing the animal requires is to bond with a master and his or her family. The puppy forgets its former home very quickly. The hunter will be able to establish bonds with his dog that will prove to be very useful when hunting.

This two-month-old Pointer puppy carries all the hopes of its master.

Indeed, the hours spent in taking care of the puppy allow the hunter to create a wonderful relationship with his new pet.

But acquiring a puppy also raises a certain number of questions. How can one be sure of the real abilities of the future dog in the field? Will it have a good nose? Will it be quick or slow? With a keen hunting instinct or only moderately interested in game? It is difficult to judge all of this when confronted with a ball of fur only a few weeks old. The puppy's body is still in only a formative state. Who can tell what it will look like a year later? The puppy's temperament is not yet fully formed either. Will the dog be tough or sweet? Of course, by observing the litter one might discern some character tendencies, but nothing is certain at this age. Moreover, the puppy's master will have to show a real ability to train it for hunting: so much more has to be done! Otherwise, the training will be done later by a professional trainer.

The sale of a full-grown dog also has its problems. Changing masters represents a real trauma for the dog and must be done with a lot of tact and patience. The dog's adjustment to a new way of hunting and, more generally, to a new way of life is not assured either. The dog will take a lot of time to develop a close relationship with its new master.

At the same time, buying a full-grown, trained dog has many advantages. The hunter has at his disposal a helper that has already been completely trained by a professional and is ready to hunt. The hunter is sure of his dog's performance because he can see it perform in the field. Of course, the rather high cost of buying a trained dog deserves some consideration. But if one adds to the purchase price of a puppy its food and lodging for a year, veterinary care, and thorough training for several weeks by a professional trainer, the amount is not appreciably less than the price of a full-grown, already trained dog. The decision, however, remains first and foremost a matter of personal preference.

Get things in writing

Settle with the breeder on a purchase price, and make it official by putting the terms of the deal in writing. This often spares you difficulty later on, should the dog prove unacceptable for health reasons or should you fail to receive all the documents promised to you. It is routine for the breeder to allow the new owner a set number of days to return the puppy if it fails a health examination by the new owner's veterinarian. Get this in writing. The terms of such an agreement should also clarify whether an ill dog will be replaced with another or if the purchase price will be refunded.

The Hunter
and
His Dog

The Puppy's Arrival at Home

Here it is! Finally, the puppy arrives home. Everyone wants to see it, touch it, and pet it. The puppy, however (here, a Brittany), needs peace and quiet above all in order to start discovering its new universe.

The puppy's first day in its new home is an important event for the whole family. Everybody is delighted, each member of the family wants to pet the newcomer, to hold it and to cajole or play with it. Voices and excitement mount, and the children's exclamations fill the air.

However, this happiness is not shared by all. The animal itself is utterly terrified. It has just been torn away from its brothers and sisters with whom it has lived since it was born. No more play or freedom from care. Driven over a bumpy road on the trip to its new home, the puppy is likely to become carsick. Upon arrival, a horde of totally unknown human beings fall upon the little dog,

screaming and lifting it up while touching it constantly. Tossed from one pair of arms to another, fear is the puppy's only companion. Stop!

The new owner must immediately put an end to this kind of behavior, which jeopardizes the puppy's integration into the new family. The key word for these first moments is peace. Stressed out by this sudden change and by the loss of all familiar surroundings, the puppy who arrives in a new home longs for only one thing: that it be left in peace. Leaving it alone will allow the animal to recover its spirits and gradually discover its new world when ready. To gain the dog's trust, perhaps the best thing to do is begin by giving it something to eat. This is the most concrete way of showing it that the new home is hospitable.

From the start, the puppy must also have a quiet place, a space where no one can disturb it. It is best to avoid using a wicker basket for the puppy's bed, which, though decorative, will be destroyed very quickly by the puppy's sharp teeth. Plastic baskets should also be dismissed from consideration because they might be uncomfortable in warm weather. Indeed, the bottom of a cardboard box cut in the shape of a basket or crate will certainly best suit the puppy. It must be padded with old sweaters. Toys are not necessary at first.

The puppy's bed should be placed in a corner of the kitchen, protected from drafts and heat sources like radiators. In order to avoid disturbing the puppy constantly, the puppy's bed should absolutely not be put in a hallway or where people walk. However, the animal must all the same be able to see the members of its new family move around.

The first night, alone and locked up in a dark room, the newcomer will truly discover what solitude means. It will probably moan, calling for company. Giving in to this is out of the question. The owner must go see the puppy and appear very angry, reprimand the animal without touching it and then leave immediately. A good trick for calming the puppy down is to put a kitchen timer with an impressive tick-tock on the old sweaters in the bed. This noise will remind it of its mother's heartbeat and help to calm its fears. The owner can also leave the radio on a station that broadcasts more words than music, to make the puppy feel less alone: to the puppy, the radio represents a human presence.

Hunters rarely keep hounds at home, which are more often destined for kennels (like these Fawn Brittany Hounds).

Some Veterinary Advice

Puppies must be regularly treated with deworming medication because they carry worms transmitted by their mother during gestation (here, a female Labrador and her puppy).

The purchase examination is a wise precaution that allows the veterinarian to make a thorough health examination of the animal.

When one purchases a puppy or a full-grown dog, it is important to go to a veterinarian for an examination prior to or within a week after purchasing the animal. First, this purchase examination allows the buyer to see if the dog has any hereditary defects that would entitle the owner to void the purchase. During the course of this first examination, the veterinarian, in consultation with the master, will also be able to select an appropriate program of vaccinations and worm treatments for the animal. This first examination will also be an opportunity for the dog's owner to ask questions of a specialist who will be sure to advise the owner.

The veterinarian will first make sure that the dog does not have any genetic defects. Birth defects are usually fatal. Some of them are visible to the naked eye of the buyer, but such defects are rare. On the other hand, the most important abnormalities are cardiovascular defects, which only a very thorough examination with a stethoscope will detect. If the animal has a chance of surviving, surgery might be considered. Other genetic defects, such as most ocular defects, which eventually may result in the loss of the dog's sight, may be detected by the veterinarian from the dog's earliest years.

Setting up a vaccination program with your veterinarian is the most important part of the initial examination.

As we have seen the law requires dog breeders to have puppies undergo initial vaccinations against distemper, hepatitis, leptospirosis, rabies, kennel cough, and parvovirus before they are sold. Most of the time, in the following weeks, a booster shot of the initial vaccinations is necessary. The veterinarian will take this opportunity to verify that the rabies vaccination mark is plainly visible, because the mark is indispensable in

proving legally that the dog has been properly vaccinated against rabies.

A large number of puppies have parasites—intestinal worms transmitted by their mother during gestation. Therefore, it is essential to treat them as soon as possible to get rid of this problem. Indeed, if nothing is done, the worms will multiply and will end up reaching the puppy's stomach, where they will inflict serious damage. Be careful! It is impossible to detect worms in the puppy's feces with the naked eye. Therefore, it is useless to wait until you see the worms in order to begin the treatment. Bring a stool sample to the doctor; the presence of worms can only be detected by microscopic evaluation of the stool.

The initial examination after the puppy is purchased also allows the veterinarian to specify the proper diet for the puppy. The veterinarian suggests

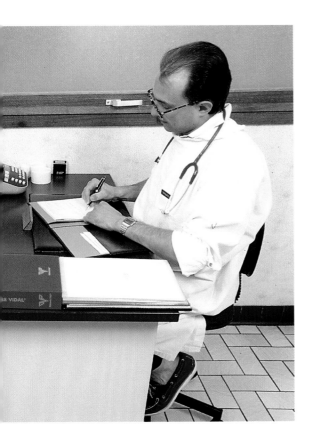

menus enriched with vitamins and minerals. He also warns the puppy's owner against the danger of bad habits, such as giving tasty treats to a puppy, and draws up a list of forbidden foods. To support this dietary advice, a program of growth and weight gain allows the puppy's master to watch over his new companion's development.

Finally, and more generally, this first consultation gives the puppy's owner, sometimes discouraged by the puppy's behavior, the opportunity to ask the veterinarian numerous questions, which will reassure the owner. Most people arrive at the veterinarian's with a veritable list of questions, proof that this professional visit is necessary.

Note: Rabies represent a significant threat to you, your family, and others. Immunization at three to six months, with another inoculation at the age of one year followed by annual rabies shots thereafter, will protect your dog from this horrible and unnecessary disease.

Remember, rabies is caused by a virus transmitted by the bite of an infected animal (bats, foxes, raccoons, and skunks, for example). Chance of survival once the virus starts reproducing within the body is extremely slim.

Schedule of vaccinations

—*Eight weeks:*
parvovirus, distemper, hepatitis, leptospirosis, rabies, and kennel cough
—*Twelve weeks:*
booster shot for the foregoing vaccinations and initial vaccinations
—*Sixteen weeks:*
booster shot for the foregoing vaccinations
—*At the end of a year:*
distemper, parvovirus, and hepatitis, plus rabies, leptospirosis, and kennel cough
—*Every year:*
rabies and leptospirosis
—*Every two years:*
distemper and parvovirus
—*Every five years:*
hepatitis
Important: Vaccinations take about one to two weeks for immunity to develop.

The Dog's Nutrition

A dog's nutrition is essential. The dog's health, as well as its physical condition and therefore its effectiveness in the field, all depend on its nutrition. Since World War II, significant progress has been made in this field. At that time, many hunters fed their dogs with a porridge made with bread and milk. They categorically refused to give meat to their dogs on the pretext that doing so would risk making their dogs feel like eating game instead of retrieving it. It is not difficult to imagine the damage produced by such practices. But above all, the dogs, physically weakened, were not able to prove their full capabilities during difficult hunting days. With the help of new studies, meat made its appearance in dogs' bowls. Then, the era of home-cooked dog food dawned, that is, food prepared with kitchen ingredients by the owner. Raw or cooked meat was mixed with cracked rice garnished with carrots. Many still feed their dog this way.

However, at the same time and with considerable resources, the food processing industry launched the production of industrial food for pets. First, there was moist food (that is canned), then dry food (of the crunchy type). The first advantage of mass-produced dog food— its practicality—did not escape the attention of consumers. There was no longer any need to buy meat or to worry about keeping it from spoiling. No more need either to cook rice and vegetables. Moreover, some hunters quickly gave up canned food for dry food because it is even easier to use.

What should one think about mass-produced dog food? You might be tempted to say only positive things. If people choose a reputable brand, the products offered are of excellent quality. The ingredients in reputable dog food are perfected according to the results of the latest studies in nutrition. As a result, meals are perfectly balanced, providing the dog with all its nutritional needs. There is thus no need to feel guilty that a home-cooked meal, though more expens-

These little Jack Russell Terriers eat out of the same bowl, so it is difficult to know if each one has actually consumed the quantity of food necessary for its growth.

ive and time-consuming to prepare, is better for the dog.

As a matter of fact, how can one be sure that the ingredients prepared at home and put in the dog bowl are perfectly suitable to an organism so different from us? Doesn't the home-cooked meal lack certain essential components, such as mineral salts and vitamins? Is the quantity of fat sufficient? Of course not. It is impossible to prepare a perfectly balanced meal by yourself. Only dietitians from large, specialized companies can do so. However, there is one reservation: meat-flavored meal used in industrial food does not require the dog to exert the necessary chewing and digestive functions. Accordingly, it is important to give the animal some additional meat from time to time and some beef bones to gnaw. There is also a range of products that offer food suitable for puppies' growth. Likewise, some dog foods are more appropriate for hunting

season, when dogs are more active, while other dog foods are better for the off-season. In addition, the veterinarian may give valuable advice by recommending one product over another and may also calculate the ideal proportions of food to give to the dog according to its level of activity and morphology.

The hierarchy of full-grown dogs often becomes manifest during meals. Therefore, it is wiser to feed each dog from separate bowls spaced widely apart than trying to let them feed from a single dish.

Dietary supplements

Is it necessary to supplement dogs' nutrition with vitamins and minerals? Absolutely, if the dog is fed with vegetables and meat or if the puppy is in full growth. But be careful! The absorption of excessive amounts of calcium or certain vitamins may be as detrimental as their deficiency. Therefore, it is important to scrupulously follow the dosage of supplemental vitamins and minerals prescribed by the veterinarian. On the other hand, nutrition based on industrial food is nutritionally sufficient by itself. No supplements are required. If a specific nutritional deficiency should arise, the veterinarian may recommend supplements on a regular basis.

Training Basics

The calmness of a dog at home, like the retriever shown here, guarantees its acceptance by the whole family. It is indeed a necessary part of the dog's training.

Two distinct stages will lead the dog to live on good terms with its human family. For the master, the most important stage is the actual training, which will allow the dog to become an invaluable helper for hunting. But if most dogs live in the field for only one or two days per month during a hunting season that lasts for four or five months, they are also pets who share the family's daily life the rest of the time. For this coexistence to be a peaceful one, the dog must learn a few basic principles, and it is training that will accomplish this.

Contrary to hunting training, which rests with a single person, general training concerns all members of the small familial community. To be completely successful in this endeavor, it is imperative that each member of the family behaves toward the dog according to the same pattern.

The most urgent aspect of this training is teaching cleanliness as soon as the puppy arrives. House training must thus be done in stages. The first thing to do is to respect the puppy's biological clock. It is generally agreed that a puppy does its business fifteen minutes after eating, so this is the best time to take it for a walk. As soon as the puppy has finished, it must be brought back home right away so that it will understand that this stroll is not a game but an opportunity to satisfy its needs. Moreover, by observing the puppy carefully for a week, you can figure out the times when the puppy's need to relieve itself is urgent. The "excursion" outside must, of course, correspond to these "strategic" moments.

Unfortunately, this is not always enough, and accidents on the floor are numerous, especially at night. The best thing to do is to put old newspapers on the kitchen floor. The puppy will have no other choice but to do its business on them. At the end of a week, it is necessary to start reducing the size of the area covered with papers. Progressively, the surface devoted to the puppy's nocturnal needs will shrink, and at the end of two weeks only a page of the newspaper will stay on the floor, on which the dog will do its business. This is the time to bring the newspaper page along for a walk with the dog. The page, put on the ground outside, will show the place where the puppy can relieve itself. There should be no deviation from this rule. If the dog is caught in the act of peeing on the carpet, stern verbal reprimands should rain down on its recalcitrant little head. There is no point in striking the dog because your tone of voice alone is more effective. Nor is it necessary to scold the dog if it is not caught in the act, because its master is the only one who knows the reason for the punishment. The practice of rubbing the dog's nose in its feces and urine is utterly ineffective. It is much better to try to catch the animal in the act and above all to encourage it with rewards when it relieves itself in the right spot—namely, outside!

Other fundamental points in training a dog are basic obedience and recognizing its name. The goal is to be able to control your dog in any kind of situation. The animal recognizes its name rather quickly, so you must repeat it often in a friendly tone of voice, while patting the dog. Congratulate the dog warmly as soon as it turns its head when someone says its name. The important thing is to choose a simple name with a maximum of two syllables that are easily recognizable and sound clear. The puppy gets used to its name more easily if you use it systematically at mealtime. Once your puppy learns its name, the way to obedience is accomplished only gradually. This training must begin inside the house. When the puppy is busy walking at the other end of the room, say its name, followed by the word "here." At the same time, it is useful to bend down and perhaps to clap your hands. Your tone of voice used should not be that of an order but rather inviting and encouraging. In most cases, the puppy rushes up and must be warmly greeted. If it does not rush up, attach a long string to its collar. The pupil is then left free to stroll about the room unconstrained. When you call its name, pull the string gently and without force toward you. Repeat the name and the word "here" over and over, without paying any attention to the dog's reticence. Once brought back congratulate it as if it had performed the exercise of its own free will. These sessions must be repeated until the dog answers to its name without fail or difficulties. Then you may do the same exercise outside. An enclosed place, such as a garden, should be chosen, and it is essential to start first with the rope, then without it. Next, do the same exercise in an open field. It is essential not to tolerate

Children play a great part in the puppy's socialization (here a Weimaraner puppy). However, it is important to watch children carefully because they may also inculcate bad habits in the puppy.

the slightest error. At the first error the string technique must be used again until the puppy responds to its name without fail.

The last essential point of basic training is walking with a leash. Before starting this training, the puppy must understand that the leash is not a toy intended to be nibbled on. On the contrary, walking on a leash is a serious exercise! The first few times, the puppy

A puppy (like this Beagle) that can be easily manipulated will likely be an easy-going full-grown dog.

Following page: Breeding several dogs together (like these Korthals or Wirehaired Pointing Griffons) makes the animals more even-tempered but requires extraordinary patience on the master's part.

will struggle with it. Then, very quickly, it will start to pull it like a mad dog. It is at this very moment that you must intervene, by giving the puppy what professional trainers call a "ringer." Pull the leash back sharply each time the puppy pulls on it. Don't keep pulling back continuously, because this will encourage the animal to continue pulling. Dogs like to pull when they feel resistance. If the "ringers" are not sufficient, it is necessary to resort to using a rolled-up newspaper. The dog is placed even with your knee as the walking

begins. Each time the puppy passes in front of your knee, punish it with a light tap with the paper on its muzzle. This tap is painless if done with restraint, but it is enough to stop the dog and bring it back. Retractable leashes should be avoided because, with their greater length, they give the dog the impression that it can escape its master's authority. It is also useful to make the dog walk always on the same side (left for right-handed persons and right for left-handed persons); this will facilitate the transition to walking next to you when you begin carrying a shotgun or rifle.

Words to tell it

Generally, a full-grown dog understands approximately twenty different commands. Each command must always be preceded by the dog's name to attract its attention. It is absolutely necessary to use the same words for the same order. The dog does not understand that "Here!," "Come!," "Come back!," and "Heel!" mean the same thing.

The tone of voice you use when speaking to your dog is crucial. Accordingly, you should not hesitate to speak forcefully, as an actor on stage, whether you are praising it or punishing it. This is much more effective than hitting because dogs tolerate pain well —as is evident from observing how dogs behave together. Indeed, dogs, which are after all aggressive creatures, do not necessarily perceive a violent act as punishment. On the other hand, any obvious sign of displeasure on their master's part affects dogs much more.

A puppy has difficulty concentrating for too long of a period of time. Therefore, it is better to practice training exercises in short sessions. The important thing is always to stop when the puppy has done an exercise perfectly. It is better that the puppy concludes each training session with a deserved success until the next lesson rather than concluding the session with a failure. There is no definite age to start training a puppy. From the first months of its life, the young dog is able to assimilate a certain number of rules.

A master may find pleasure in his dog's noisy display of affection. The rest of the family and guests might not enjoy these as much.

The rest of the training is simpler. The "sit" is easily achieved by pushing on the dog's hindquarters while repeating the command "Sit" or "Stay" until the animal assumes the desired position. Hold your open, flat hand in front of the dog's face as you say the command.

To teach the dog how to lie down on command, you first start with "sit" followed by the lie down position. To achieve this, pull the dog's front paws forward with your right hand, while pushing on the dog's head and back with your left hand. "Lie down" must be repeated continually and the dog must remain in the correct position for a few seconds. If it wants to immediately get up, push it down again and say "No!" or "Lie down!"

The Dog's Behavior

In order to live in perfect harmony with your dog, it is important to try to understand it. This understanding will often allow you to act accordingly in a specific situation. The main weakness of dog owners is to attribute attitudes and behavior of a human baby to their puppy. This anthropomorphism is the source of serious misunderstandings between the dog, which tries to make its master know what it wants, and the human being, who cannot find an explanation for his dog's behavior in any catalog of human behavior. If you want to understand your dog's reactions, you must try to think as it does, putting aside your own human thoughts. This is what you might call canine psychology.

Before anything else, it is advisable to understand the concept of the pack, which influences the dog's whole life in a house. Like wolves, dogs are animals meant to live in a group. In the wild, they live in a profitable collaboration: one dog can seize large game with the help of the pack's other members. This organization is also more effective when dogs face danger: by joining forces, dogs may defend themselves more easily. The links that exist between the members of this structure are complex. Hierarchy governs the whole group and prevents the pack from undergoing constant conflicts. This hierarchy expresses itself in a system of ranks given to each member of the pack. The authority that some have on others consolidates the whole pack.

Dogs instinctively need to live in a pack, but the constraints of modern life prevent all but very few people from having more than one dog at home. Thus the animal will naturally transfer this need of being in a pack onto people. To the dog, the family members become members of a pack—the dog's pack. The animal finds itself in a social structure in which it feels at ease. This feeling determines all its behavior toward the people who surround it.

However, for a dog to be happy among the pack, it must have a place, a well-defined rank within the hierarchy. The master hunter becomes the head of the pack automatically because he is the one who leads the fundamental activity of the dog: the hunt. The other members of the family will occupy inferior ranks, the dog putting itself last in this hierarchy.

But it is not always obvious to the animal to occupy this last place. The dog may indeed be a domineering male, endowed with a strong personality. It will constantly want to climb the rungs to reach the position that it covets so much: leader of the pack. If there is no strong authority on the master's part, the dog very quickly becomes the leader, which will lead to many problems. Then, by

A puppy's training is accomplished as much by words and tone of voice as by gestures (here, a small Labrador).

having its way, the animal will refuse to obey. The dog might also become aggressive and readily bare its teeth, even with family members. Fortunately, such headstrong behavior is relatively rare among hunting dogs, but it is nonetheless advisable to be on guard against such behavior because it can appear anytime.

To avoid these excesses, the dog must feel the authority of the pack's leader. Having an assertive master allows the dog to find a clearly defined place within a group, which provides it with a sense of well-being. If a dog is not subjected to any authority, it will not be happy because it absolutely needs to belong to a pack with

This small Golden Retriever's games are not innocent; it is advisable to take advantage of them in order to facilitate the dog's training.

a hierarchy. The dog's slogan could be "Each in his own place."

In daily life, the dog assumes the same relationships with the family's members as one finds within a pack. For instance, playing is not at all innocent because it allows dogs to defuse situations of potential conflict between two members of the pack. Thus, when a dog plays with a child, it tries to gain the upper hand in order to avoid any

confrontation. However, it must be clear that a dog mimes these scuffles with children not only for the simple pleasure of fighting. The dog is testing its "adversary," gauging the adversary's weak points as well as its own. For the dog, it is a way of testing the rigidity of the hierarchy to see if it would not be possible for it to gain a position at the heart of the pack. This is why dogs like to play all their life.

The pack represents one of the essential structures of a dog's life and psychological balance. No problem for these black-and-white Great Anglo-French Pointers, but an isolated dog will always consider the humans around him as his pack.

Dogs express submission (or domination) toward humans according to a well-defined code. Forced to submit, a dog will probably content itself with bending its back and flattening its ears to avoid meeting its master's gaze. If the submission is truly sincere, the dog might go so far as to lie down on its side, exposing its belly and genitals by raising a back paw. By exposing a part of the body that is particularly sensitive and vulnerable, the dog puts itself at the mercy of those who dominate it—be they humans or other dogs. This position is characteristic of total submission. In general, the dog comforts itself in this submissive position because it will be rewarded with a pat. The dog is always looking for emotional and physical contact with the human beings who share its life—a result of the dog's acceptance of its master as the pack leader. It is also a way

This Basset Hound shows its submission by exposing to its superior (dog or human) its belly, a particularly vulnerable part of its body.

Are dogs able to sense what is going to happen?

A lot of masters think that their dog "senses" when they are going to leave for a trip or when they are going to leave their dog alone. They also feel that the dog knows when it has made a mistake. These feelings are not attributable to some "visionary" abilities on the part of the dog, but to the dog's interpretation of certain signs. Thus, the dog who grovels before its master is probably unaware that it made a mistake because it does not remember it anymore. On the other hand, the dog knows that it is punished each night when its master returns home. The dog no longer remembers that it relieved itself on the carpet during the day. Only the master notices it upon returning home. The dog knows only that it is time for its

"thrashing"! As for sensing a departure, obviously dogs spend their time observing us and very quickly learn to spot the slightest changes in our behavior. But it is more likely that a dog will simply be agitated because it is able to perceive our own change of mood. Indeed, the dog does not understand that we are leaving for a trip, but it certainly realizes that our state of mind changes as the time to depart approaches, and this change in our mood causes the dog anxiety without its knowing necessarily what this means. The same is true of the dog who "senses" that the opening of the hunting season is coming. In fact, it is the increasing nervousness and excitement of its hunter-master that makes the dog feel a form of anxiety.

for the animal to tighten the bonds with the pack's members. Some studies have shown that a simple pat radically lowers dogs' heartbeat and blood pressure. Patting calms them down and reassures them. With their master, dogs also repeat the behavior they displayed as puppies with their mother. They often sleep by resting their head on the feet of a person whom they care for. This behavior is similar to that of dogs in a pack who will gladly sleep piled up on top of one another. This is certainly reminiscent of puppies' behavior: a brood always sleeps against the mother's belly, the puppies piled up pell-mell.

When a dog meets one of its own, on a sidewalk for instance, the determination of the hierarchy occurs according to various criteria. Either the dominant and the dominated appear clearly, or there is an apparent equality between the two dogs. In the former case, there is no fear of confrontation. The weaker dog (who is not always the less physically strong) expresses its submission to the other one immediately. In the latter case, two situations may appear. If neither of the two dogs really wants to dominate the other, they start to play, or else they part, completely indifferent to each other. On the other hand, if both want to dominate, they will redouble their threatening behavior and will try to impress each other. Often, this bluff suffices to discourage one of them, who will then act submissive. If such is not the case, a confrontation might ensue. But it is important to know that most dogfights are due to the behavior of their owners. A dog kept on the leash will feel assured by its master's strength. Indeed, a dog that is naturally submissive risks wanting to become domineering if it thinks that it has its master's support. Most of the time, it is better to let the dogs settle their relationship between themselves and to intervene as little as possible. Masters who feel compelled to intervene at all costs risk unleashing a conflict between the canines.

Today we are too inclined to forget that dogs remain animals whose actions are dictated above all by wild instinct. Therefore, as often as possible, we must try to understand how the dog would react in a given situation if it were still a wild animal in a pack. This will allow us to explain many types of behavior among those who share our homes today.

Artesian Bassets of Normandy at play. Fights between dogs are rare as long as humans don't intervene. Most often, dogs establish hierarchical relationships among themselves without conflict.

The Fundamentals of Training

Pointers: Encouraging
the Passion for Hunting

The puppy is in the process of changing completely into a full-grown dog. By living close to people, it has learned the rudiments of a harmonious family life. Serious matters may now begin; the initiation to hunting may start. The training of a pointer is a delicate task that requires the utmost patience. If the hunter does not have enough land at his disposal or if he does not have the necessary skill, he should seek the help of a professional trainer. For others, before starting the training, it is important to know a few simple rules that will spare them from making some serious mistakes.

Contrary to common belief, it is not discipline that makes a good pointer but rather its passion for hunting, and everything must be done to encourage this passion. The more the dog appreciates what it is doing, the easier it will be for it to accept the behavioral constraints that its master imposes on it. Accordingly, the first step consists of developing this passion of hunting in a young dog. This should be done as soon as possible: a four- to five-month-old dog is perfectly capable of understanding what game is.

For this first step, the captive-bred quail or similar type bird is the most suitable species. The bird should be hobbled with an easily visible string several yards long in order to slow the bird down. It won't be able to fly very far and will therefore be easier for the young pup to find. This result may also be achieved by trimming the bird's wing tips with a pair of scissors. The young dog must be led close to the quail, which will inevitably take off under the dog's nose and settle a little farther away. Nearly all puppies are unable to resist such a temptation. Accordingly, the dog will start to chase the quail, to cause it to take off again, and so on. It might even be able to seize the bird. The passion for hunting is born at this very moment. It does not matter whether the dog does not stop, or whether it starts to pursue the bird, or even if it catches the bird. The important thing is that it keeps a positive memory of this first contact with game. At this stage, there is no need to try to inculcate some kind of discipline in the puppy. The act of seeking and finding its prey must be its sole guide. However, this session must occur only once or, at the most, twice. Then it will be time to proceed to the next stage.

Many dogs are afraid of the sound of a gunshot. Unfortunately, this fear, for which the hunter is almost always responsible, is very difficult to eradicate. However, there is a simple method for managing this fear. Every meal should be accompanied by the firing of a small-caliber pistol. The firing, which is not very loud, should occur the moment the puppy receives its bowl of food. Very quickly, the

The use of a rope allows the trainer to master the dog's different stages of pointing: here, an English Setter in full training.

Now, the pupil may be put in contact with a bird that flies unhindered. As usual, the dog will want to. pursue it. The dog must be led in front of the game by fastening a long rope to its collar. It is important to know exactly where the bird is located. The dog will use its nose to ferret out its prey. When the pupil arrives close to the bird, the master must hold the other end of the rope, while leaving the dog free to move. When the bird flies away, the dog will want to pursue it. It is then imperative to restrain the dog with the rope firmly but without violence. The dog must always be praised for his work. The next step consists of stopping the dog with the rope before the bird flies away. This must be done as gently as possible so the dog will not interpret it as a punishment. It is very likely that by the end of two or three sessions of this kind, the dog will end up stopping without the master intervening. The bird's taking flight must then be punctuated with a gunshot to which the puppy is already accustomed.

For this kind of exercise, it is especially important not to use pheasants because these birds often run and are likely to frighten the puppy with their considerable size. It is better to use quails or young partridges whose feet have been previously hobbled to prevent them from fleeing.

It is also important to finish these exercises as soon as the dog has found the bird and stopped. There is no need to repeat the sessions, which are in fact opportunities for the dog to make mistakes. It is better to leave the dog with a feeling of success.

To teach a puppy how to point, some hunters use a fishing rod with a bird's feather attached to the end. The hunter then wiggles the fishing rod in front of his pupil's nose. Although this method produces some

pupil will associate the sound of a gunshot (so long as it is not too violent) with something pleasant. Afterwards, more powerful guns must be used to produce a louder noise. However, it is important to avoid taking the puppy trapshooting under the pretext of wanting to get it used to noise; the results are often catastrophic.

good results, it also produces a serious problem that is not without consequences. Enticed in such a manner, the puppy gets into the habit of pointing only at game that it sees. Only the animal's appearance and its movements arouse the dog's excitement. The puppy thus neglects using its nose to find and point at its prey. There is a great chance, then, of seeing such a dog searching for future game through vision rather than smell.

Obviously, all the training described above requires that the dog must first

Opposite: Accustoming a dog to the sound of a gunshot is a very delicate process that must be done as gradually as possible. This English Setter puppy is in danger of becoming gun-shy.

Below: The crucial moment of training: this young English Setter discovers game for the first time.

POINTERS: ENCOURAGING THE PASSION FOR HUNTING

Training a Springer Spaniel to quarter is similar in many respects to training a Pointer.

learn all of the basic training techniques, *especially* coming when called. A disobedient dog is useless for hunting. It is therefore useless to start any other kind of training before the dog learns to come back when called.

As soon as a dog knows how to point game using its sense of smell and how to come back at its master's call, it is finally ready for his first hunting trip. Then, it is imperative to instill in the dog a deeply rooted passion for searching for game. Above all, one must not try to teach the dog maneuvers such as quartering a field in a zigzag pattern, the "down" position, or forced retrieving at this stage. The dog will perceive these constraints, which it is unable to understand at this stage, as unnecessary annoyances that will only dull the joy of hunting. This premature teaching might, as a result, even diminish the dog's effectiveness. On the contrary, for the first trip, the puppy must feel free to run to its

heart's content and understand the goal of hunting: seizing a bird with the close collaboration of its master. This first hunting trip must be done under very specific conditions. Group hunting, in which several dogs are used, must be avoided at all costs. The hunting trip should last only a few hours so the dog will not feel overly tired. Finally, game should be relatively abundant so the dog will not be discouraged. To achieve these conditions, it is better to hunt alone during the day. During this first trip, the dog will certainly make many mistakes and forget some of its brief training. This is not important. The only thing that matters is that the dog gets passionately fond of hunting. There will always be time to return to lessons that the dog has forgotten.

After this first exposure to hunting, the dog may proceed to the second stage of training.

It will probably be necessary to review pointing training, again with the help of a rope. But from now on, it is time to train the dog to search for game in a more orderly manner. To do this, the hunter must face the wind in a field. Then he should run in a weaving fashion, encouraging his dog to run with him. With each turn, the hunter will whistle twice. Gradually, the hunter will escort the dog less as it quarters. The hunter will make the dog turn at his order always by whistling. Finally, after a few sessions, the hunter will not have to run with the dog anymore.

After teaching the dog to quarter a field, the hunter should then teach the animal the "Down" command. First, the hunter gives the order to the dog to lie down, forcing it to assume the down position—that is, lying flat on its belly, with its head flat on the ground between the front paws. The order "Down!" is repeated several times while holding the dog in the correct position. A good way to make the dog learn this command faster is to do the exercise before feeding it. The dog will understand quickly that it will be fed only after assuming the down position. Many hunters feel very proud when their dog does a perfect down, although this exercise is relatively easy to achieve. In the field this order is very useful. It helps to stop a dog from pursuing a deer or from crossing a road. Some sensitive dogs do not tolerate this very strict position well. With such dogs, the hunter can be satisfied with a "Sit" position, because what really counts is that the dog stops dead in its tracks at once on command. Once the dog masters the down position in front of you, move

The electronic collar—pros and cons

Many hunters wonder about the electronic collar. Fixed in the dog's collar, it is a device that discharges a mild electrical shock. The trainer discharges the shock by means of a hand-held transmitter. It has the great advantage of punishing a dog at a distance without its understanding the relationship between the punishment and the master. Thus, the punishment comes at the moment when the mistake is made and often when it would otherwise be impossible to punish the dog because of the distance between the animal and its master. This immediate punishment is extraordinarily effective. The electrical aspect of the collar is a little frightening, but one must realize that dogs have a less sensitive skin than ours. This method is therefore not dangerous to the dogs' health. However,

some dogs that are too sensitive do not tolerate the electrical shocks, and these collars might cause the dog to freeze up. In such cases it is best not to use the collar. Moreover, the very effectiveness of this training tool may lead to harmful results. For example, if the dog is punished at the very moment it smells a woodcock, it might lose forever the initiative essential to any hunting dog. Accordingly, caution must be exercised in using this tool, which may be beneficial or harmful depending on the person who uses it. If the training is a success, the dog should welcome the electronic collar just as it welcomes its master's gun or boots. This sort of reaction means that the dog has not received more than three or four electrical shocks during its entire training.

The "Down" command, impressive though it may be, is not very difficult to teach; it is more of a mechanical skill than real training.

farther and farther away from the dog while repeating the command so that the dog stays in the position. If the dog moves from the spot, don't hesitate to come back and put it in the correct position. This exercise should be repeated often until a distinct stop is obtained from a considerable distance, with the dog waiting for its master to come before standing up. The "Down" command may be associated with the harsh and long blast of a whistle and accompanied by a characteristic gesture, such as raising both arms. In the field, the dog will more easily understand the order when given this way, especially when it is far from its master.

For some hunters, retrieving is of prime importance, while for others it is secondary. The main problem for a dog retrieving is that it might want to break its point to catch the prey. It is therefore important to wait until the dog points perfectly during an entire hunting season before asking it to retrieve. Fortunately, a dog often retrieves game naturally. If it refuses to do so, there are methods called

"forced retrieving," but the results are very uneven and opinions are divided about these methods. If a dog is determined not to retrieve, it is better to train the animal how to point dead game by using specific signals, such as asking him for a new point or to "lie down" in front of the animal. The dog must also learn how to creep as soon as the hunter orders him to do so. Indeed, the dog must break its point to move forward slowly toward the game and point at it again. Here again, many dogs will do this naturally if they are encouraged with only a pat or a few words from their master the moment they point. But this takes time to perfect.

Passion is the key word for training. A dog is capable of great prowess and initiative if it is enthusiastic about hunting. Only the dog who know hows to find rare and difficult game and how to point such game to allow its master to shoot it deserves the name of hunting dog. The others are merely show dogs politely repeating their lesson!

Retrievers:
Working on the Dog's Instinct

Training a retriever is very different from training a pointer. A retriever's main work occurs after the game is shot because the retriever is above all meant to retrieve. However, a retriever puppy should learn the same basics as any other hunting dog suitable for small game. When a retriever puppy reaches the age of six months, it walks well on a leash without pulling and always stays on the same side of its master. The puppy also knows how to sit on command and, of course, to come back to its master when called. Finally, like a pointer puppy, the young retriever has become gradually accustomed to the sound of gunshot at mealtime. It is imperative that all these points be perfectly assimilated before starting the actual training for hunting.

The first step consists of training the dog how to stay. When a duck passes by or a pheasant beats its wings, the dog should not disturb the master or under any circumstances the hunting that is taking place. This lesson is taught using two precise instructions. The first one is heeling without a leash. The trainer leads the dog slowly while repeating the "Heel!" command. As soon as the pupil looks like it is about to deviate from heeling, a light touch with a rolled-up newspaper on the dog's snout will put it back in the right direction and position. This exercise is relatively simple to do if the dog has been thoroughly trained in walking on a leash.

A retriever also must learn how to sit on command. The puppy has already learned it, but now it is time to perfect the position. Strolling with his dog, the master stops and orders the puppy to sit by saying "Sit." Then the order "Okay" may be given to release the animal. Once the puppy is sitting, the master must gradually move away while repeating the "Sit" command. If the dog gets up, it must be

Following pages: Ideally, no obstacle should slow down a retrieval.

This Labrador proves that the instinct of retrieving is present in almost all retrievers from the earliest age.

Marking

This primitive term refers to an ability typical of retrievers. These dogs can in effect memorize visually the points at which different pieces of game fall. Thus, at their master's command, they can fetch wounded birds by running back and forth without forgetting a bird. This visual memory can be improved through training. The dog is put in the "Sit" position, then several bumpers are thrown at it before sending it off to retrieve. No bumpers should be forgotten. In practice, some retrievers stay at the hunter's feet, memorizing the drop spots of a good ten ducks. Then, as soon as the hunter gives his command, the dog fetches the ducks one by one, sometimes even in the order in which they fell.

Above: The bumper launcher is a kind of gun that releases a bumper made of fabric and rubber and is used for retrieving exercises.

Opposite: Retrievers trained only with bumpers may have some difficulty in switching over to retrieving shot game.

put back in the correct position at the same place, and must start the exercise again. The goal of this exercise is to succeed in maintaining the dog in this position until ordered to leave the position with the command "Okay!" Then the dog must be ordered to assume the "Sit" position again and maintain it while being enticed by some temptation, such as with a toy that the dog can fetch only on command. The same training can be used with the dog's dish. The puppy must remain seated in front of its bowl without throwing itself upon it, until released by the command "Go." This discipline is absolutely indispensable when the dog is hunting. Indeed, the dog should know how to remain absolutely immobile in front of a duck that flounders in the water.

Only the hunter may command the dog to fetch the duck, at a favorable time, when the dog will not disturb other hunters.

The next step consists of teaching retrieving. Most retriever puppies with a good pedigree already have the instinct to retrieve. Very often, they retrieve a stick or a ball that their master has thrown to them. It then becomes necessary to refine this retrieving to make it more effective.

To do this, the puppy is put in the "Sit" position. A bumper is thrown out quite far but in plain view. The pupil is maintained immobile by the command "Sit," then sent off to retrieve by the command "Fetch." Quite often, the young retriever plays with the bumper instead of retrieving it at once, twisting and turning around. In this case, the dog should be tied

to a thirty-foot-long rope (ten to twelve meters). Once the dog is ordered to retrieve, the master holds the end of the lead. As soon as the dog seizes the bumper, the master brings the dog back directly and firmly. After a few sessions, the dog will lose the habit of making detours. Once the dog is by its master's side with the bumper in its mouth, the lesson is not altogether finished. The dog should release the bumper at the command of "give." If the dog resists, the best remedy is to pinch its ear, which makes it immediately let go of the object. The dog should not drop the bumper before being in front of the master nor should he put the object in the master's hand. If the dog does not perform this task correctly, the master should send it off to fetch again until the object is retrieved

The Labrador's role is not to flush the upland game in front of the master. Therefore, the dog has to stay staunch when a pheasant or a duck flushes.

properly. The master should never be satisfied with a half-done exercise because the dog will quickly become quite mediocre.

Training gets more complicated when the bumper is thrown without the dog's seeing where it falls. To do that, the trainer starts with a simple exercise. The dog should be placed behind a low wall that blocks its view. Then the bumper is thrown about 30 feet (10 meters) away from the dog. Gradually the exercise is made more challenging by throwing the bumper farther and farther away, especially into bushes where the dog will not be able to see it. This forces the dog to use its nose to find the object. The trainer will help the dog by giving it hand signals indicating the direction and the distance of the object. Eventually, the dog will end up understanding these signals.

The retriever shows its full abilities in the water. Most of these dogs love water and do not have to be begged to jump in. Accordingly, it is easy to make them retrieve an object thrown in a pond or a river. If the dog shows reluctance to get wet, the bumper should first be thrown just in front of the dog in shallow water so the animal will put only its paws into the water. Then the trainer may increase the distance progressively to force the dog to swim.

Once the dog retrieves the object correctly, the exercise should be repeated several times using the head of a game bird. Initially it is better to choose small birds to make the dog's task easier.

A retriever should also be able to find a bird that has been winged but that has escaped. Therefore, it is important to teach the dog how to find the track of a bird. This is done by tying the head of a game bird to an improvised fishing rod and dragging the game over the ground about 30 feet (10 meters) out of the dog's sight. The trainer then brings the retriever to the beginning of the trail and lets it try to follow the scent. The dog will not fail to put its nose on the ground and will follow the trail until the game is found.

A retriever (here, a Golden) should go into the water making the least splashes possible so as not to startle the game.

Spaniels: Channeling the Passion

Spaniels are dogs with a promising future, especially in Europe. Indeed, the reduction of hunting grounds and changes caused by evolving land use has led to new practices to which spaniels have adapted very well. These dogs always stay close to their masters. They know how to explore the most difficult terrains inch by inch, retrieving wonderfully in the water as well as in thick brush, and they always chase game within gun range without stopping.

Choosing a puppy is a very critical time for the hunter. These dogs already have considerable natural aptitude for hunting, so they do not need extensive training as long as they come from a genuine working breed, which is often far from being the case. Even more so than with pointers, choosing a spaniel with a well-established pedigree ensures success and will simplify training.

Like other types of dogs, the spaniel must learn how to retrieve without fail. It should also know how to walk on a leash and not be afraid of gunshot, before going on to the actual training.

At first, as with the pointer, the master should develop the dog's passion for hunting game. Ideally, the master should find a deserted location where there are a lot of rabbits. These sites can often be found in inactive industrial sites where there is no hunting. With a two- to four-yard-long rope (about three meters), the

The boundless energy of spaniels, as with this Springer, requires considerable tact from the trainer, for he must channel this energy without suppressing the dog's own initiative.

master walks his dog at the time of the day when rabbits are most active. They will not have to wait very long before crossing a rabbit trail. Inevitably the puppy will break into pursuit of the animal. It is absolutely essential for the master to run with his dog and, if possible, try to spot the game before stopping his dog. At the end of a few sessions, the master will be confident that his dog has developed an eager passion for pursuing game.

The second important point of training a spaniel is the "Down" command, traditionally replaced by the "Hup" command with spaniels. As with pointers, the "Hup" command is the way to stop the spaniel from a distance if necessary. It also allows the hunter to stop a dog on the wrong trail of a rabbit, a hare, or even a deer. It is also the more reliable way of slowing down a dog that goes too far away. Game that is flushed and missed should not be pursued, and the "Hup" command allows the hunter to avoid this

problem. There is no point in using the "Lie down" command instead of "Hup." A simple "Sit" command will suffice. The hunter may practice this command before feeding the dog so the dog learns the command more easily. Once in the field the hunter should practice walking the dog again on a lead behind the game. When a rabbit or bird flushes, the dog should be quickly trained to stop flushing with both the help of the lead and the "Hup" command. Later the exercise should be repeated without the lead. After a few sessions the dog should be able to stop at the "Hup" command and let the game go free. Retrieving may be taught to the spaniel in the same way one teaches a retriever. However, a spaniel will not be able to "mark" game, and its overall effectiveness in retrieving might accordingly be less than that of a retriever.

With Springers and retrievers, retrieving should be worked the same way. However, these two dogs will not show the same sense of marking game.

Leading the hunter to game by barking

Some spaniels bark when they flush a rabbit, pheasant, or woodcock. Although trainers generally do not encourage hunting dogs to bark, a well-timed one can be very valuable in densely wooded terrain and in thickets, where it is impossible for the hunter to see the dog, even though it might be only a few yards away. In such terrain, the dog's barking allows the hunter to prepare to shoot. Thus, instead of trying to correct this little impulse of enthusiasm, it is better to cultivate it as something precious.

Hunting with a couple of English Springers can be very effective in dense undergrowth.

Hounds:
Rigor and Discipline

Although numerous handbooks on dog training are available, there are no very modern handbooks on hounds. Moreover, we believe, no professional trainers for this kind of dog exist. Perhaps for this reason, many dog lovers believe that hounds do not need to be trained. If this were true, the youngest dogs in a pack could look only to the example of older dogs for training. This belief is completely false, as one look at a pack coming back at night will show: half of the dogs missing will be found later all over the surrounding countryside. Another pack might also simultaneously flush three or four different species of game.

A hound's training is indispensable. Hunters who lead stag hunts know this perfectly well, and it is for this reason that their dogs are perfectly trained. For hounds intended for hunting small as well as big game, following a few training rules will improve the hunt.

The first stage of training is obedience. Like a pointer, a hound is also perfectly capable of obeying its master, but life in a kennel does not facilitate lasting contacts with the master. As we have seen, a dog needs its master's presence to be effective at hunting. It is therefore important to spend as much time as possible with the dogs.

As soon as they arrive at the kennel, the hounds should be capable of responding to their name and obeying the "Here" command as any other dog would do. The method to use is always the same. Nonetheless, the "Here" command must still be perfected. The dog must also get accustomed to the sound of the horn that will be used later in the forest to recall the dogs over long distances.

Once a dog knows how to obey its master, it must learn obedience within the pack. This should be worked on at feeding times. Dogs should eat only when they are ordered to do so and not before. Once the dogs have learned this, the hunter may go out with the pack, which will follow behind him in a well-organized group. This exercise should be repeated as often as possible to accustom the dogs to move together in an orderly way.

The second step is training hounds how to find and follow the scent of game while barking and how to track only one species of game. This must be done in a place where a large number of animals can be found. However, before undertaking this training, each puppy's desire to track game must be developed. For that, the puppies, one by one, may track the simple scent of a piece of meat. In France, for example, hounds are called "declared" when they are able to flush and follow the scent of game while barking.

Ideally, hounds should be trained using the game that they will hunt later.

A two-month-old Basset Hound puppy. Contrary to widespread opinion, hounds do not train themselves. The hunter must inculcate in them the same discipline imposed on other hunting dogs.

Then it will be easier to train the dogs to hunt only one species of game, while ignoring the scent of all other game. For example, some hounds specialize in hunting hares or wild boars, while others hunt wild boars and foxes.

To prepare the dogs for their future task, the dogs must be taken to areas where game that they should not hunt are plentiful. The hunter must stop the dogs firmly as soon as they pick up the scent of

such forbidden game. Here, previous obedience training will help a great deal. Next, the hounds should be given the sought-after game and be allowed to trample, bite, and sniff it. The dogs then should be lavishly praised.

This method is not infallible, but it is the only one likely to yield favorable results if done with perseverance. Generally, patience is the key in training hounds.

Under their master's lead, these small Blue Gascony Hounds learn how to avoid the snares involved in following a scent. The best way to train hounds is to work the young ones together without the presence of fully grown dogs. In that way, the young dogs will develop their own sense of initiative and will avoid relying on the older dog's greater experience.

Bloodhounds:
Patience and Experience

Without a doubt, the Saint Hubert is gifted with one of the finest sense of smell. By virtue of its strong nose, it is of tremendous help in searching for blood of wounded big game.

Training a bloodhound is a long-term and exacting process that should not be undertaken lightly. Only several years of training will produce an effective bloodhound. Also, before deciding to purchase and train this type of dog, the hunter must be sure he will be able to take the dog on a minimum of twenty hunting trips a year. That being said, choosing the breed still

remains. The bloodhounds known in Europe as the Bavarian and the Hanover are considered the best, but the conditions for obtaining them are very strict and few puppies are available. French Basset Hounds are also good bloodhounds, as well as certain bigger hounds, like the Saint Hubert. But the most commonly used bloodhound is the Dachshund. It might not be very big, but it is highly effective. Generally, German Pointers are also excellent bloodhounds.

Tracking represents the basis of a bloodhound's training and should start during the dog's earliest years, by forcing the puppy to search for its bowl. In the garden, out of the dog's sight and with a handful of scraps, the trainer lays out a ten-yard long (about ten meters) straight trail, at the end of which he hides the bowl. The pupil will therefore use its nose to find its meal. Discovering its bowl is the best reward. Generally, the trail should be made more difficult to follow: longer, more circuitous, and over, under, and through obstacles. The trainer should also lay out the trail earlier and earlier before the dog's meal so the scent is more difficult (but not too difficult) for the puppy to follow. Simultaneously, as with any other dog, basic obedience must be taught to the bloodhound and, like retrievers, it must learn to heel without a leash. And, of course, the puppy must also become accustomed to gunshot. The bloodhound's actual training can then begin.

With the use of congealed blood from a deer, the trainer lays out a trail in the forest. The blood is poured into a plastic bottle, such as an empty bottle of

mineral water. The lid of the bottle is perforated to let the liquid flow out rapidly, drop by drop. The trail is then laid out using the blood, while the skin of the game is dragged along the ground parallel to the blood trail. The important thing is to lay out a straight trail approximately ten yards (ten meters) long. The dog should be brought on the field right away. After having followed the trail, it will find the skin of the game, which should contain a piece of meat. Very gradually, this trail should be lengthened. The drops of blood should be spaced farther apart on the ground, except at the end of the trail where the drops should be more concentrated. The interval of time between when the trail is laid out and the dog's arrival should also be increased.

At the end of a year, the trainer should advance to a trail several miles/kilometers long that he will set out not less than twenty-four hours before the dog arrives and even during rainy weather. It is useful to scatter pieces of paper on the trail at regular intervals so the hunter will be able to follow the dog's progress more readily. This also enables him to spot the dog's hesitations and mistakes more easily. The trail should contain numerous difficulties: it should turn upon itself, cross the trails of other animals, form right angles, and so on. At the end of the trail, the hunter should not forget to reward the dog accordingly. The dog should also learn to bark when it has found a wounded animal. In fact, when the game is located, the dog should not be on a lead or check line. The dog's barking will allow the hunter to be led to the game more easily. To train the dog when to bark, there is a relatively easy exercise: the dog's bowl should be filled and put in a tree, while the trainer repeats the "Bark" command. This same command should then be given when the dog is in front of the skin of a deer.

These are but the basics of training a bloodhound. For advanced training, one should consult a specialized manual.

The Bavarian Bloodhound, along with its cousin, the Hanover Bloodhound, is the only real, exclusive specialist for tracking blood.

Terriers and Flushing Dogs: Obedience and Control

Hunting big game is on the rise in France. The main technique in that country is to use noisy flushing dogs. Hunters use short dogs, such as terriers or Basset Hounds. Like any other dog, flushing dogs must be trained to become really effective. They will also receive a complete training with a special emphasis on the obedience of the "Here" command. Indeed, this discipline is extremely important for flushing dogs. It must be acquired by working on three different commands. Obviously, each dog should be trained how to recognize its name. Obedience in a pack should then be worked on so the dogs learn how to return to their master on command. Finally, they should get used to rallying upon hearing the blast of the hunting horn. This is always difficult to achieve because these dogs are often stubborn. However, if the hunter follows the advice given above, the desired results will not be long in coming.

The taste for tracking must be developed by applying the same method as the one used with hounds. All the same, with certain exceptions, there is no need to teach flushing dogs to track only

Most terriers, like this Jack Russell, are very obstinate, which calls for constant firmness on the master's part.

one type of game because they hunt all types of big game.

On the other hand, it is imperative to train the dogs how to stop systematically as soon as they come upon the trail of an animal. For that, the master needs the help of another person. This person will stand on the trail, while the master brings his dogs through the brush to the trail. When the master approaches the trail, he gives the "Stop" command to his dogs. At the same time, the other person firmly pushes the dogs back toward their master. Then during the hunt, all hunters in the area should be instructed to stop the dogs using the same command as soon as the dogs come upon the trail. If this rule is respected, the dogs should stop on trails without continuing to flush the game.

A "bloodhound" terrier?

It is altogether possible to train a terrier like a bloodhound. In fact, in Germany, during official field trials, terriers are supposed to accomplish the same tasks as bloodhounds, namely, following an artificial trail for several hours. The Jagd Terrier is perfectly fit for this difficult task. However, it is best to avoid having this dog hunt with other flushing dogs if you want it to be truly effective when searching for large wounded game.

A pack of Fox Terriers can be extremely effective when hunting big game, provided they always obey their leader.

Dog Shows and Competitive Events

What is the Purpose of Competitive Events?

Previous pages: Before the beginning of a difficult tracking of black grouse.

Jean-Pierre Rolland (left) with "Brack," from the village of Bois Sauvages, and Francis Maudet with "Calin," from the small farmhouse of Eyraud, two very great champions from the early nineties.

There are two main competitive events for hunting dogs: the field trials and hunting tests. There are field trials for pointers, retrievers, and spaniels, as well as for hounds; even underground and above-ground events for terriers. Dachshunds and bloodhounds also have specific competitive events in which the dog's ability to perform in the field is demonstrated.

These different events are supposed to put the dogs in situations most similar to the those they encounter on the hunting field. One or several official judges preside over the trials. During these events, official prizes recognized by all professionals from the hunting world are rewarded to the best dogs; in the United States the titles awarded are Field Champion and Amateur Field Champion.

Although the methods of these dog shows and competitive events are very different, the goal is always the same: selecting the most effective dogs objectively so that they may be used as choice breeding dogs. Such champions thereby contribute to the improvement of their breed.

Spaniels, retrievers, and pointing breeds (in the United States) are also eligible to participate in hunting tests. These breeds are evaluated on their hunting ability. AKC regulations call for three levels, with each succeeding level increasingly difficult. Dogs that successfully complete these three levels earn titles Junior Hunter, Senior Hunter, and Master Hunter, respectively.

Contrary to popular belief, the pointer can be highly effective in hunting woodcocks. It can even win a field trial using this difficult bird.

What are Field Trials?

Field trials are competitive events for pointers, retrievers, and spaniels, and they are specific to each category of dogs.

Field trials fit for pointers are surely the most important, judging from the sheer number of participants. There are three big competitive events for pointers, of which the spring field trials are the most prestigious. In the wide grain fields of France, for example, (essentially the Beauce region), the best professional trainers and amateurs come to pit the finest pointers against the gray partridge. Within fifteen minutes, the dog has to find the pairs of partridges located in the field where it hunts. It must point the birds and wait for its master's arrival. Then the master will command it to creep toward the game, which then flies off. The dog should stay staunch after the bird is airborne. The leader shoots with a blank cartridge revolver to simulate gunshot and then joins up with the dog. If the trial as described seems simple in theory, it is another matter

In many countries field-trial judges are volunteers who devote countless hours to a process that helps improve breeds. Following the dogs in all kinds of weather, for entire days, is not an easy task.

in practice. The prey is difficult and wary. Located in open cornfields, it is able to see danger coming from far away. Also, a dog might make many mistakes. The judge will be there to appreciate not only the quality of the dog's work, but also the specific style of each breed. In short, this first field trial requires incomparable qualities from the dog, and only the best ones succeed in these challenging conditions. Dogs that are selected are then gathered in the evening to present the winners of the day. But before

winning the title of Field-Trial Champion, a dog must win many other victories. Indeed, it must participate at stakes. In stakes, two dogs compete against each other. They must run the same field trial as in the individual field trial described above, except that they attempt to outperform their adversary. They must also respect the other dog's point if it is the first to point game. In the spring, dogs compete equally in two disciplines: quartering—dogs make 100-yard (about 100 meters) runs—and big

The different competitors and judges gathered at an altitude of 6,000 feet (2,000 meters) at a field trial using black-cock at Chatel, in the region of Upper Savoy in France. This trial, organized by the English Setter Club, is one of the more selective field trials in France.

The green "carpet" of the Beauce region is used for competitive events during spring field trials. The contrast between the bright green and this mahogany Irish Setter is stunning!

quartering—the ultimate trial where dogs make 300-yard runs! Pointers are the undisputed kings of these latter trials and only English Setters can compete with them. During these field trials, dogs from other European countries do not run with English dogs.

The Shot-Game field trials take place in the fall, under conditions comparable to the field trials described above, but the dogs hunt over less extensive distances. These trials use planted pheasants, birds surely easier to hunt than the wild part-

ridge! The bird is shot in flight and the dog must retrieve it flawlessly. As for spring field trials, individual and paired competitions are organized, but the big quartering event is not a part of the competition. Some of the competitive events using woodcocks or snipes are clearly more difficult.

It is important to point out again some of the field trials using mountain game. These trials are also very difficult because of the terrain and the ferocity of the game, which is not shot.

Summer field trials represent the last category. They belong to the Shot-Game field trials, but captive-bred quails are most frequently used. As a matter of fact, these trials are for beginners who wish to start competing.

Field trials for spaniels are modeled on Shot Game field trials for pointers. However, rabbits are the prevalent game in these trials. These competitive events are very selective because not any dog that comes along can make a small animal break cover from impenetrable thornbushes!

Field trials for retrievers are more complicated simply because of the specialization of these dogs. Retrievers are put in the conditions typical of battue hunting of pheasants. They have to mark where the game falls and fetch the game on command while doing a perfect retrieval. Either the masters use a leash in a French-style trial, or the dog is left free in a British-style field trial. Needless to say, the latter is the more arduous. Moreover, retrieving in the water is required.

Nowadays, field trials are undergoing increasing criticism. They are blamed, in particular, for artificially producing competitive dogs that no longer bear a relationship to practical hunting dogs. Many hunters also assert that it is impossible to hunt with a champion dog. For the most part, this criticism is unfounded because dogs that win field trials are almost always excellent hunting dogs. In general, field trials are extremely selective and prizes are rarely given to usurpers. One must not forget that the goal of these competitive events is to elect champion dogs for breeding purposes, capable of producing first-rate hunting dogs.

"Sacre du Petit Monastère" (Consecration of the Little Monastery), one of the greatest English Setters of the 1980s, was led to the prestigious title of Champion of the Big Quartering by Jean-Paul Koumchasky.

A Few Words About
Dog Shows

A champion title or a prize always turns the master's head more than the dog's.

In addition to field trials and hunting tests, there are competitive events in which the beauty or conformation of hunting dogs is what counts. These exhibitions attract large audiences. Dogs are presented to a judge who measures the contestants against the official standards of their breeds. They are classified by breed, usually into three categories. The first one is working dogs, for dogs over fifteen months of age that may have already won field trial competitions or working tests, and whose masters also want them to win a prize in a dog show. This ultimate award is required for official confirmation of the title Field Champion. The second class is for young novice dogs, nine to eighteen months, and the last is the class for puppies, six to nine months old.

As already stated, at the show the dog owner has to present his animal before special judges who will evaluate the dog. The dog is required to stand still without sitting down. It should not make a lifeless impression, but wag its tail happily in its breed's typical fashion. The dog has to put up with being touched all over, and has to allow, for example, its teeth to be checked without difficulty. It has to walk at its owner's side without jumping up in the air or pulling at its leash. All these things have to be practiced before the dog's owner can take part in a show. Club members who are old hands at showing dogs will surely be glad to give colleagues and their dogs the necessary guidance.

Equipment for the show should include food and water dishes, a normal leash, show lead, brush, chamois cloth, mat for the dog to lie on, and hand towels. Food, water, dog biscuits, and whatever is necessary for the presentation in the show ring, are needed. Documents such as the vaccination certificate, a copy of the

pedigree, copies of any titles awarded and any working tests passed, and confirmation of the dog's entry in the show, should also be brought.

In general, however, dog shows are not very useful for hunters, and their only purpose is to provide visual gratification. Certainly, it is necessary that dogs of a specific breed do not deviate too much from the official breed standard. But it is quite impossible to think seriously about producing dogs that combine great effectiveness with irreproachable esthetic qualities.

Choosing a dog is done by choosing either the best hunters or the most beautiful animals. How can one believe that by systematically choosing dogs with the best hunting abilities, these dogs also will be the most beautiful? A dog that combines beauty and hunting skills is only the result of pure luck.

For the uninitiated, the customs of a "show ring" are often totally incomprehensible. Long experience is necessary in order to appreciate all the fine points of dog shows.

Licensed Trials
for Hounds

In various European countries, for example, hounds have their field trials: Licensed Trials. As with field trials, the dogs are put into conditions that simulate actual hunting conditions. Each owner presents a pack appropriate to the type of game hunted. There are five kinds of certificates obtainable—rabbit, hare, fox, deer and wild boar. The owner has an

allotted time period (between one and two hours, depending on the type of game) in order to prove the mettle of his pack. From three to six judges follow the hunt either on foot or horseback. The judges are supervised by the president of the jury. When the pack is first presented to the judge, the dogs are graded according to how closely they conform to the

The judge evaluates the performance of each dog in a pack. He can identify each one according to the different colored collars.

official standard. Afterwards, the action may begin, and the owner is free to use the field as he sees fit. The fields are generally well stocked with game, which allows the pack to be put before fresh trails. The judges evaluate the coordinated action, speed, and control of the pack in grading the qualities and shortcomings of the pack. In addition, the dogs must perform obedience, barking, and smelling tests. The pack is also judged on its cohesiveness and on the ability of its members to rally. Each dog receives grades corresponding to these different criteria. If the total exceeds a hundred points, the judge awards a licensed trial certificate with honors (good, very good, or excellent). If a hound receives two licensed trial certificates, plus a title in a dog show, it is entitled to obtain the title of Field Champion.

The Licensed Trial is a spectacular and selective field trial, but largely unknown to the public.

Terriers and Bloodhounds: Their Distinct Field Trials

In Germany, France, and the Netherlands, among other countries, terriers and bloodhounds compete in very different field trials. For terriers, there are "digging" trials that simulate as closely as possible the conditions for hunting foxes underground. For this trial, artificial foxholes are constructed of timbers laid end to end and buried in a shallow trench. The top of the trench is open, allowing the dog to enter the trench. The dog traverses this burrow into which a fox is placed. The dog must drive the fox back and hold him at bay. There are also "natural foxhole" trials that take place under rather similar conditions. A foxhole is located in the countryside and the dog is unleashed. The rest takes place as in foxhole hunting, with the exception that judges are there to evaluate the dog's work.

In all these cases, the dogs must show good biting, courage, and endurance, but also carefulness. Recently, another trial for terriers was organized in France, called the Overland Chase. It is true that these dogs are increasingly used for battue hunting of

Artificial foxhole field trials pit underground hunting dogs against foxes, but without any actual confrontation taking place.

larger game. What was lacking previously was a field trial to test dogs' abilities in this type of hunting. This gap has now been filled. The dog must be able to track the scent of larger game, find it, flush it, and bring it to a designated line. The dog must also show obedience and stop on command as soon as it crosses a line, to avoid disturbing the hunt.

Field trials for bloodhounds take place on artificial trails. These trails are prepared twenty-four or forty-eight hours in advance and cover a distance of at least one kilometer (over half a mile). The trials are divided into several levels of difficulty in tracking in which the dog must pick up

an animal's scent which leads to the piece of a large animal. The dog may compete in the "howler" category—liberated from its leash, it must fetch dead game alone—or in the "indicator" category—it goes back to its master after having found the piece of an animal. In each of these two trials, the work done in tracking game is the same, but each trial is graded separately, without regard to the dog's final overall results.

These very technical trials are organized by the bloodhound owners in collaboration with clubs devoted to promoting a particular dog breed, which provide the necessary hunting grounds.

Trials for bloodhounds take place on artificial trails established several hours before the trial begins. Specifically, organizers of these events lay out a trail by dribbling drops of blood over a long distance the day before the competition or even earlier.

*N*owadays, there are more than seventy breeds of hunting dogs. They are presented here according to their country of origin. All dogs ultimately trace their origin to a single source because hunters from England, France, Germany, the United States, and elsewhere produced these dogs based on a national and specific conception of what hunting and hunting dogs ought to be. Thus, one sees that all British dogs have common characteristics, as do French, German, or American dogs.

Pointers

The Origin
of Pointers

As many illustrations prove, the Italian Hound is undoubtedly the pointer that most closely resembles the hounds that were used in the Middle Ages.

The use of pointers is surely not as ancient as that of hounds, whose origin predates Antiquity. Pointers, on the other hand, did appear during the Middle Ages. At that time, there were only two types of distinctively different pointers, because no one yet talked in terms of breed. The first type was the Pointing Spaniel; the second, the Pointing Hound. For these two dogs, the hunting technique was the same: catching birds, especially partridges, with the help of a net. The dog would find and point a covey of partridges and thereby give the hunters enough time to catch the

partridges with a net, either on the ground or when the birds took flight. Very quickly, these dogs became tremendously effective, and they became renowned all over Europe. European monarchs used to reserve exclusive usage of these dogs to themselves.

At the same time, agriculture made strides, and with it the population of small game, favored by the cultivation of grains, also grew. Oysel dogs, helped by birds of prey such as falcons and goshawks, were used for hunting partridges by pointing. All the nobility began to enjoy the pleasure of hunting, and it is they who started what we call breeding today. They selected types of different dogs and crossbred them to obtain more effective and more beautiful dogs. The idea of breeding was born.

The advent of firearms marked a decisive turn in the pointer's evolution. Birds of prey were replaced by arquebuses, and hunting evolved very gradually to become the sport we know today.

European monarchs were especially fond of hunting pheasants. Beginning at the time of the French Revolution, pointers fell into relative oblivion. But not until the nineteenth century was cynophilia (or "enthusiasm" for dogs) born and with it the development of small game hunting and these invaluable helpers—the pointers.

Pointers, like this French Spaniel, were originally called Oysel dogs and were first used for hunting partridges by net, but above all to point birds in flight.

Evolution of Pointers
up to the Present Day

Today's preferences and those of the past

If one compares illustrations from the beginning of the century to current photos, one notices that breeds of pointers have undergone important morphological changes. As a general rule, dogs used to be heavier, but, breeders wanted to develop a more effective breed by improving their speed, which undoubtedly led to the gradual lightening of the weight called for by the breed standard. However, esthetic considerations also played a role.

Contrary to what its appearance might lead people to believe, the Korthals, or Wirehaired Pointing, Griffon appeared recently.

For a hundred and fifty years, pointers have experienced profound changes linked to two criteria: the evolution of the landscape and new hunting practices. At the end of the nineteenth century, many European countries were very different from contemporary Europe. It is interesting to turn over the pages of the illustrations and the first photos from this period to realize the amazing changes that the landscape has undergone. The countryside was composed of small fields devoted to subsistence farming. Small plots predominated, with a different crop grown on each. Each farmer jealously guarded the hedgerows that delineated his piece of land. Small thickets were present everywhere. The landscape, broken up into such small plots, allowed game to find cover in numerous places. Although game was more abundant than today, it would be a mistake to think that these fields were carpeted with hundreds of young partridges! On this subject, collective memory is subject to gross exaggerations.

Nowadays, the countryside suffers from the changes that land has undergone. Small plots have been regrouped into huge fields and hedgerows ripped out. In some places small farmers raise only a single crop, such as wheat or corn. Moreover, farmers systematically resort to chemical products, weed killers, or chemical fertilizer. This change of the rural landscape has therefore not been favorable to game. However, it was not entirely responsible for the near disappearance of hares or partridges. Today, with a little effort, it is still possible to find areas where these game are abundant.

Confronted with these changes in land use, the practice of hunting has also evolved. Dogs have become faster and bolder because it is not easy to point partridges in vast, plowed-under wheat fields. Dogs have gained in effectiveness because they were obliged to hunt considerably more difficult game. Our grandfathers' spaniels and hounds would probably look pathetic in the plains of the Beauce region of France today, which have been totally denuded of hedgerows and copses! Breeds that have learned how to adapt to this new situation have achieved a big success with hunters, while breeds that have not have gradually faded away.

Faced with this evolution, each country has perfected its own strategy. The British opted for extreme specialization and focused on the qualities of four breeds of pointers. The Germans chose versatility over specialization. In France, each region preferred to keep its own breed that would fit to both a specific hunting style and a particular kind of terrain. It is these different approaches that have produced the diversity and richness in the world of pointers that we currently enjoy.

The Future of Pointers

Blue Picardy Spaniels are the typical example of a breed that has been abandoned by hunters whose preferences have evolved. Dog breeders, who did not know how to improve this breed, are partly responsible for this disaffection.

In England, Germany, and the United States, the use of pointers is on the upswing. Pedigree dogs are becoming more popular, which proves that hunters are increasingly attracted to this type of helper. The Brittany and the English Setter are the leading breeds, closely followed by the Pointer, the German Shorthaired Pointer and the Korthals Griffon, or Wirehaired Pointing Griffon, as it is known in the United States. One might conclude that the future of pointers is very promising, yet, a more astute analysis shows that the conditions in which these dogs hunt are deteriorating. A pointer should be able to hunt difficult game over a relatively vast area occupied by one or two hunters. But, such uncrowded conditions are becoming, at least in Europe and in some areas of the United States, increasingly difficult to find. The cost of leasing hunting fields has increased sharply. Hunters are therefore obliged to share the cost to be able to rent an area, and that area is likely to be quite limited in extent. Indeed, they often hunt standing in line with all their dogs, and this inevitably degenerates into disorder. Dogs envy each other, break each other's points, and steal game from each other. To avoid such disorder, hunters are obliged to "break" their dogs, forcing them to hunt under the gun, which takes away the initiative that distinguishes pointers.

Woodcock hunters and their dogs

Pointers, in particular English Setters, have benefited from the expansion of woodcock hunting. Woodcocks are the last truly wild game that can be hunted in certain countries by a lone hunter and his dog. However, there are certain problems. Due to the growing popularity of woodcock hunting, it is uncertain whether the species will be able to survive for very long.

Today, most of the time, pointers are used like spaniels, even like retrievers. From this rather unfortunate evolution, a misunderstanding has arisen between breeders and hunters concerning the actual character of the dogs to breed. Dog breeders strive to produce dogs that conform to the official standard of the breed. Pointers are thus likely to win the competitive events that re-create ideal hunting conditions, but pointers bred in this manner no longer correspond to the hunters' needs. Most of the time, hunters are satisfied with dogs that have a moderate gait, that do not disturb nearby hunters on their line, and

that are able to hunt only pheasants recently released from captivity. As a result, misunderstandings arise between the world of dog breeders and that of hunters. But solutions do exist. If hunters want to continue hunting in line, they should choose dogs better suited to this style of hunting. On the other hand, managers of hunting areas might want to re-create hunting conditions that are favorable to the use of pointers. These dogs then will be able to express their skills fully. However, this solution is possible only if the cost of renting hunting areas is lowered.

Thanks to the efforts of enthusiasts, the Brittany is living proof that a small regional breed may become one of the leading breeds of pointers worldwide by corresponding perfectly to hunters' tastes.

French Pointers:
Adapting to the Soil

No other country has as many breeds of pointers as France. France opted for a way of development very different from that of its neighbors, Germany, England, or Italy. The explanation for this diversity of breeds lies in the variety of hunting practices encountered in France.

Ever since firearms have existed, French hunters have practiced random small-game hunting. Alone or with other hunters, the French hunter strides along his territory carefully searching for game with his pointer. The animals that the hunter will encounter are very diverse: hares, rabbits, red or gray partridges, wood pigeons, thrushes, ducks, woodcocks, larks, and pheasants, which were relatively late to appear in French game bags. French hunters take pleasure in this diversity and the surprise that comes from it. The French hunter likes this type of hunting perhaps more than any other European hunter. He is the only one to decide which distance he will cover according to his inspiration. A small field, a hedgerow, a thicket, a pond—this is what random hunting is all about. Today, it is true that the landscape has changed. Some regions underwent significant changes due in particular to the reallocation of land. However, in many places, the appearance of the French countryside remains quite varied and more traditional than in other countries to the detriment of French agriculture, but for the happiness of hunters who do not live in regions with a large production of grains.

Another characteristic of French hunting is the extreme diversity of landscapes. How is it possible to compare hunting in the marshlands of the Somme region with hunting in the sun-drenched hills of the south of France? France, a vast country in the eyes of other European countries, has an extraordinary variety of climate and topography. Thus, French hunters developed habits that are specific to their region and that cannot be transplanted anywhere else.

French pointers are the result of the combination of all these factors. The diversity of French breeds is as rich as the diversity of French regions. Ten breeds of pointers exist in France.

Unlike foreign breeds, the names of French pointers evoke a very specific region: Picardy, Brittany, Auvergne, Bourbon, Ariège, Pyrenees, Gascony, Normandy, and Ile de France. This proves how deeply rooted each breed is in its own region.

From two large types of pointers, hounds and spaniels, local hunters gradually molded different dogs in order to respond to specific needs based on terrain, climate, or game. Until recently the lack of good roads and the enclaving of certain regions favored the maintenance of this diversity—one that is still reinforced by a very French parochial spirit. Indeed, for a long time, the hunter from the Auvergne region wanted to hunt only with an Auvergne Hound. This chauvinism was present in most regions of France.

Other European countries developed a totally different policy. At the beginning of the century, a period during which dog breeding experienced a big rise, German, British, and Italian hunters focused on three or four breeds and tried to improve

them by selecting breeds at a national level, thereby replacing local breeds with national ones.

This movement, common throughout Europe, did not happen in France, where each region jealously kept its own breeds. The big drawback of this conservatism was to limit the selection of the best sires in each region. In fact, it is easier to find unrivaled dogs in the kennels of an entire

country than in the kennels of one province.

Breeders of other countries have beyond all question succeeded better than French breeders in the evolution of their breeds of pointers. These more effective breeds ended up invading French hunting grounds, whereas French pointers have not taken over other domains. Thus, many French hunters chose the English Setter, the Pointer, the German Shorthaired Pointer or the Wirehaired Pointing Griffon, and rare was the German or British hunter who opted for a French breed. The only exception was the Brittany, which is discussed later in this book. Nevertheless, this dog was less common abroad than English or German dogs were in France.

Today, French breeders have modernized and improved their breeds according to new demands. They have adapted to hunters' needs by taking into consideration the changes brought to the landscapes.

As a general rule, French pointers, those versatile helpers, are able to assist the hunter in his multiple tasks during a day of random hunting. But if French pointers hunt outside the limits of their region of origin, they still show characteristics appropriate to their region. Compared to the overspecialized British dogs, French pointers are rather "generalists" that are able to point a covey of partridges or flush a rabbit from cover, as well as retrieve a duck or flush thrushes.

French pointers are generally supple, resourceful dogs that adjust easily to new situations. Created to hunt in varied surroundings, they usually walk at a moderate pace, exploring the terrain methodically. They are not sprinters but rather quick walkers. In general, their quartering is not very wide, which is considered by some hunters as an advantage, by others as a defect. However, it is important to be careful with French pointers because certain breeds have been crossed with British breeds. The different crossbreedings altered the temperament unique to these dogs, and it is not unusual to see them hunting like their parents from beyond the English Channel. For these reasons, a considerable number of French dogs cannot be considered truly French.

Although the Blue Picardy Spaniel adjusted well to marshland hunting, it was not able to avoid the competition of foreign breeds, especially with the Labrador.

French Spaniels

There are five large breeds of French spaniels, all of which originated from the pointers of the Middle Ages. Certainly, spaniels from France go back to the Crusades: the crusaders had brought hounds that were crossbred in the Middle East with local long-haired Greyhounds. But the more recent distinction of breeds dates from the last century. At that time, English hunters came regularly to hunt in France, especially in the sandy moors or the marshlands of Brittany or Normandy. They brought along their dogs, generally spaniels or setters that were left to board with farmers along the coast of the English Channel. The numerous crossbreedings with local dogs gave birth to the Brittany and the Pont-Audemer Spaniel.

The Blue Picardy Spaniel is a more recent breed. It is a variety of Picardy Spaniel obtained by crossbreeding with the Gordon Setter. The Picardy Spaniel is an exception because it did not receive any direct contribution of English blood. It was developed from a cross between French spaniels and local sheepdogs. The French Spaniel remains a close descendant of the spaniels from previous centuries that were used for hunting with a net.

As one can see, the concentration of spaniels along the coast of the English Channel (in Brittany, Normandy, and Picardy) is not a coincidence. Surely, French hunters wanted to take advantage of the setters' qualities and of other spaniels from the other side of the English Channel, whose superiority must have been undeniable at the time. Indeed, it is difficult to imagine how hunters from Brittany or Normandy would have let their dogs throw in their lot with British dogs if they had been much better hunters than their English counterparts. Besides, if British hunters used to bring their dogs along, it is because they knew that they would not be able to find good hunting dogs in France. This fact clearly suggests that French and British breeding practices differed during the second half of the nineteenth century.

The French Spaniel

For a long time, the French Spaniel has been the archetype of the spaniel from Continental Europe. More imposing and heavier than other spaniels, it remained, until recently, very close to spaniels born

The French Spaniel, one of the most ancient of spaniels, scarcely betrays its regional origins.

Currently, there are two tendencies among breeders of French spaniels: those who wish to produce a light and fast dog and those who opt for a more original and more bulky form to the detriment of the dog's speed.

during the Renaissance. Like them, it possesses a certain number of qualities that assure its success. First and foremost, the French Spaniel has great courage: it will not shrink from thorns or any other obstacle. Methodically, the dog explores each inch of land slowly, without tiring. Indeed, it is not a great galloper but rather a persevering dog with stamina. It is also an excellent retriever that establishes a close relationship with its master. In the 1970s, however, the French Spaniel underwent a significant change. Some breeders introduced a lot of blood from English Setters and, to a lesser extent, from Brittanies in order to improve the speed and nose of the French Spaniel.

Strengthened by these crossbreedings, the Brittany was able to compete in field trials with other Continental European dogs. The results were not long in coming: French Spaniels ascended to the highest steps of podiums at award ceremonies. However, this tendency was denounced by those who wanted to keep the original type. Some made fun of this new spaniel calling it a "British Spaniel" or "French Setter." Even today, there are two very distinct French spaniels. One is fast and light, with an acute nose, while the other one is clearly heavier, less fast, but more diligent.

What is one to think about all this? It is simply not possible to preserve a breed indefinitely as it has "always" been. Inevitably, crossbreeding occurs to improve the qualities of a breed. But it is dangerous to misuse crossbreeding because the character inherent in a breed might be lost, and the breed may thereby become a mere shadow of itself. It is better to practice crossbreeding very conservatively in order to improve dogs' performance, while preserving the characteristics of the breed.

The Brittany or Brittany Spaniel

While the evolution of the French Spaniel cannot properly be called a real success, that of the Brittany has been triumphant. The Brittany was introduced into the United States in 1931 and officially recognized by the AKC in 1934. From 1934 to 1982, the breed was registered as the Spaniel, Brittany. In the opinion of the AKC, the breed is setterlike in the way it works game, and in appearance it is smaller than the setters but leggier than the spaniels. It also has a short tail and a characteristic high-ear set. As of September 1, 1982, the breed's official AKC name was changed to Brittany. In France, the Brittanies number in the tens of thousands and rank first among hunting dogs used in France—and various other European countries, for that matter. The Brittany owes its success to a unique alchemy in the history of dog breeding. A farm dog that belonged to Breton farmers (Brittany is a French province) in the last century, it was crossed with Springer Spaniels and English Setters belonging to British hunters.

These diverse crosses improved the indigenous Brittany farm dog's speed, style, and nose, while maintaining its clever and resourceful side as a farm dog. These apparently contradictory origins that combine British aristocracy with common sense would have not been sufficient to make the Brittany Spaniel a successful dog if dog breeders from Callac, the cradle of

Nothing in particular predisposed the Brittany to its success compared to other French spaniels, except the strenuous work of enthusiasts.

Following pages: The Brittany in all its splendor—the tremendous "game-finding machine." Here, it hunts woodcocks of its native region.

Contrary to what many hunters think, the coat of a Brittany is not necessarily white and orange. This photograph of puppies amply shows the diversity in the coat of this breed.

the breed, had not had the determination and foresight to allow the perfect evolution of this small dog. This handful of enthusiasts knew how to modernize the Brittany Spaniel gradually and adapt it to new hunting conditions. Today, it is a fast dog, but not too fast. Gifted with a strong nose comparable to the British dog's, the Brittany can hunt fast without danger of overrunning game. Very well balanced, the Brittany is not an inconstant and capricious star. It is an extremely effective hunting machine. All terrains, from bare plains to

sandy moors, suit it. Sly, it knows how to adjust quickly to a new situation, proof of its common sense. The only thing that one might reproach it with is its stubbornness. But this small square dog breathes vitality and a healthy state of mind. Thanks to this successful evolution, the Brittany is one of the rare Continental European dogs that will be able to adjust to the fetching of wild game in the landscapes of the twenty-first century. Moreover, the whole stock is remarkably homogeneous: there are no big differences between individual dogs. All of

them have the same appearance and give the same performance. Let's not mince words: the Brittany is the supreme French hunting dog. Other national breeds cannot compete with it.

In the field, the Brittany has a gallop with a distinctive vivacity. Its pointings, much more assertive than those of other French dogs, look a little bit like those of the Pointer. The temptation to resort too often to crossbreeding the Brittany with the English Setter has disappeared today, and selection for breeding purposes is

Above: The Brittany's vivacity and its spirit of initiative often make all the difference in the field.

Opposite: Although the Brittany is considered a woodcock hunter, woodcock hunters seem to prefer the English Setter.

done within the breed. A word of caution is called for, however. This resolutely modern dog must be used under specific conditions that allow it to develop its ample and fast quartering. Thus, it is not the appropriate dog for the very leisurely and placid hunter. To allow the Brittany to show its full potential, it must hunt difficult game over vast areas. It is also better to hunt in small hunting parties with this dog and to avoid group hunting altogether.

The Picardy Spaniel

The Picardy Spaniel is the typical example of a very regional French pointer that was able to keep the characteristics of its origins. Native to the Somme Valley and the surrounding areas, it is rarely found outside this area. This spaniel is a great specialist of marshland hunting. For a long time, hunters used it as a helper for waterfowl hunting because they needed a dog that could withstand the worst weather and one that could retrieve shot ducks from freezing water. This dog also had to be able to walk for long hours in the mud of marshlands, retrieving teal or flushing a rabbit or hare. Nor could it be fearful of sneaking up behind young partridges in the open field or hunting woodcock in thickets. Finally, this dog had to be capable of remaining staunch for long hours to wait for the end of a passing of ducks.

The Picardy Spaniel is the result of crossing French spaniels with farm dogs of the Picardy region in northern France. Originally, at least, British blood was not used as it was with other spaniels. Today, this dog is distinguished from other short breeds by its real hunting qualities. Even though it is almost impossible to find it outside the limits of the Somme region, the Picardy has an excellent reputation among local hunters, and many small breeders contribute to maintaining its working qualities, not merely because of national

The Picardy Spaniel, largely confined to the limits of its native region, nevertheless meets with real success with hunters from the Somme region, in France. This allows it to withstand the onslaught of foreign dogs.

competitive events but according to their own criteria based on the dog's actual use in the field. This selection process has produced a perfectly well-balanced dog. An honest worker, the Picardy Spaniel does not hunt too quickly. Rather, it is a robust dog that has a true love of hunting. In short, it is recommended to all those who are looking for a rigorous helper and a dog that is easy to raise.

The Blue Picardy Spaniel

The Blue Picardy Spaniel is one variety of spaniel from the Picardy region that was produced by crossbreeding with the Gordon Setter. This infusion of English blood gave it great olfactory skills, a heavier frame and a British gait, but it remains above all a Continental dog confined to the Somme region. The Blue Picardy Spaniel has nearly become extinct several times. It owes its present existence first of all to the determination of certain breeders who were concerned about maintaining the breed and, second, to the desire of a few hunters to own a rare dog. However, one wonders about the real possibilities of selection in this breed. Indeed, how can one choose the stud that brings together the greatest number of working qualities when only a few studs are available for breeding at all? Breeders have to breed all

The Blue Picardy Spaniel was not as lucky as the Picardy Spaniel. Its success was always limited, even in its native region.

Today the Pont-Audemer
Spaniel is treasured: on
average, there are fewer
than ten births per year.
However, in the last century,
these dogs were numerous
in the Seine estuary.

of the dogs to maintain the effective ones, which makes any serious selection imposs-ible. Only a few dogs will be very good hunters when they are born of question-able unions. Moreover, the Blue Picardy does not have the local popularity of the Picardy Spaniel among hunters, which might have contributed to its remaining a rustic and local hunting dog.

The Pont-Audemer Spaniel

In the last century, several dozens of breeders of Pont-Audemer Spaniels could be counted in the town that gave this breed its name. Today, there are only a few of them left. Dog lovers of the nineteenth century described this spaniel as an excep-tional hunting dog—courageous, with extreme endurance, like an unrivaled retriever that is easy to train. It is not difficult to imagine the abilities of this spirited dog that is descended from the Picardy Spaniel and the Irish Water Spaniel. But, after almost a century of desperate struggle to prevent its disappearance, what remains of the Pont-Audemer Spaniel? The rare dogs that are still bred cannot restore this breed to its former splendor.

Should one try to save a breed at any price, or is it better to regard its disappear-ance as a natural process that corresponds to a change in the expectations of hunters? This question may be asked with respect to the Pont-Audemer Spaniel. Besides, it is quite difficult today to talk about the qualities of a breed when so few of these dogs still exist. Just because a particular dog may be brilliant, this is no guarantee that other dogs will behave the same way.

Without doubt, resorting to other breeds to maintain the continuing viability of the Pont-Audemer Spaniel clearly transformed this dog: it has lost many qualities specific to its breed.

French Hounds

Continental European hounds are the ancestors of all pointers. In the Middle Ages, they were among the first dogs used for catching partridges with nets or with birds of prey. For a long time, their use was reserved for noblemen because their incredible abilities to find and point coveys of partridges made them the terror of small game. Hence the many pictures dating from the Middle Ages and the Renaissance showing hounds at the sides of lords. Later, when hunting started to reach other social classes, breeds of French hounds rose in popularity and diversified. These dogs illustrate perfectly, even more so than spaniels, the hunters' determination to own a breed fit for local hunting conditions. One might also note that almost all of the native regions of French hounds are located south of the Loire River, while the regions located farther north developed spaniels instead. This phenomenon is altogether logical: hunting territories in the south are more vast and comprise large areas with relatively few marshes. Also, the warmer climate in the south better lends itself to the use of a shorthaired dog. In short, one can say that French hunters from the north of France chose longhaired dogs, whereas those of the south chose shorthaired dogs.

The French Pyrenees Hound, lighter and faster than the Gascony Hound, exemplifies the successful evolution of an old Continental European breed.

Most French Hounds have remained typically Continental European dogs that hunt with a slower gait and always close to the hunter. However, there are two exceptions to this rule: the Saint-Germain Hound and the French Pyrenees Hound.

The French Hound

The French Hound is undoubtedly the ancestor of a lot of Continental European

The French Gascony Hound attracts hunters less and less, in spite of the efforts by the dynamic club of this breed to promote this dog.

Following page: The evolution of the French Pyrenees Hound is linked to a policy of judicious re-invigoration in which the German Pointer and the Pointer had their say! But the French Hound did not lose its soul as a result of this policy.

hounds. Its origin is very ancient. This breed includes two types of dogs, which is unique in dog breeding.

The first, the Gascony, is an animal born from the plains of the southwest. It is still an imposing dog, even if it has lost some of its heaviness. Close to the original French Hound, it is a calm and quiet dog that does not have excessive energy, but has important physical abilities. It hunts at a trot, exploring the terrain methodically without ever straying too far from its master. In a word, this dog is best suited for hunters who do not wish to have a dog with too much vigor and initiative. Instead, this dog is for calm hunters. The French Gascony Hound, losing popularity, attracts only a small number of hunters, despite the enormous efforts made in its favor by the club devoted to promoting this breed. It probably no longer suits the hunting practiced today. This dog also has difficulties adjusting to the new developments of the French countryside where wild game have become a rare commodity.

On the other hand, the other French Hound, the French Pyrenees, is an unquestionable success. Smaller and lighter than the Gascony, it is also faster and has a more ample quartering. It is a more modern variety of the Gascony because it has beyond a doubt benefited from infusions of British (Pointer) or German (Pointer) blood. However, modernization has not denatured this dog. Indeed, today it holds the same place among French Hounds as the Brittany holds among French spaniels. On the other hand, the French Pyrenees Hound is a little harder to train than the original French Hound and training requires a certain adroitness.

Nearly absent north of the Loire River, the French Pyrenees Hound is a big success with hunters from the south of France, because of its legendary resistance to hot weather. It is a practical hunting dog, effective and rustic, able to master the most difficult game. Its points are perhaps not spectacular, but they are reliable and its retrieving is often impeccable.

Like the Brittany Spaniel, the French Pyrenees Hound, is an example of an ancient Continental European breed whose evolution has been perfectly successful.

The Auvergne Hound, a relatively traditional dog, is very popular among hunters.

dog was very successful in the first half of the twentieth century. But its heavy gait and short quartering undoubtedly led to a certain disaffection on the part of French hunters. One might be surprised not to see this dog in its native region anymore.

The Auvergne Hound appeals to the hunter of small game who wants to have a calm and all-around dog. With good reason, some blame it for being a bit stubborn. Although truly effective only after a few years, its training does not cause any problems and it is suitable for a novice hunter. Displaying emotions openly, the Blue Auvergne knows how to make its master fond of it and does not try to fool him. If a hunter wants a calm and diligent dog, he might choose a Blue Auvergne Hound, but if he wishes for a more unusual dog, he would be better off with another breed.

The Bourbon Hound

Here again is a French breed that fell into oblivion and is not well known by the general public. It owes its survival to a handful of enthusiasts and persistent breeders. Originally, local hunters wanted to have at their disposal a good all-around dog, perfectly suited for a specific environment. For a long time, the breed remained within its regional borders, then hunters nationwide discovered the amazing rusticity and efficiency of the Bourbon Hound. Thus, this breed spread over the whole country. Its effectiveness was maintained at a respectable level until World War I. But the war destroyed all the breeders in the north of France. At the end of the war, some amateurs had a very hard time trying to re-create the breed, but this exhausting work led to nothing because World War II struck a fatal blow to the Bourbon Hound.

The Auvergne Hound

More recent than the French Hounds, the Auvergne Hounds are the descendants of pointers from the island of Malta. After their order was dissolved, the knights of Malta brought pointers back to France and established them in the farms of the Cantal region. In this region, the color black is often called blue, which accounts for this breed being called Blue Auvergne. Adjusting to difficult terrains, this rustic

In the 1970s, a few "archeological" dog breeders, who took historic illustrations as models, claimed that they had re-created the breed from a few dogs found here and there in the region from which the Bourbon Hound originated. Nevertheless, it is extremely difficult to consider these dogs as genuine Bourbon Hounds when nobody can say for sure what a Bourbon Hound looked like. Moreover, crossing a Brittany with a German Pointer may produce offspring that perfectly match the description of the small Bourbon Hound. Does reproducing the appearance of an extinct breed matter as much as re-creating the appropriate temperament of that breed? Is it not an illusion to want to revive a breed at all costs when the hunters themselves condemned the breed to disappear by taking no interest in it? These questions remain unanswered. In his book, *Les Braques (The Hounds)*, A. L. Blat wrote in 1986: "It is better for breeders to let the fossils sleep and to put their efforts into selecting among the mainly effective breeds in our country." These are words full of wisdom in our view.

The Saint-Germain Hound

In his kennels at Saint-Germain, King Charles X owned a pointer bitch imported from England who answered to the name of "Miss." The king crossbred her with a French Hound. The puppies born from this union were all white and orange with a pink nose. Hence, the breed of Saint-Germain Hound and also its common nickname "half-blood."

The dog was a little plump, with short quartering and rather frail. But it had an excellent nose. At the beginning of the century, the arrival of masses of British dogs supplanted the Saint-Germain Hound to a limited extent. He reappeared just before World War I, in part by riding the wave of the rising popularity of pointers in

The Bourbon Hound disappeared entirely during World War II. Are dogs that carry this name today real Bourbannais? The question is worth asking.

Following pages: A Brittany and an English Setter retrieving a woodcock. These two breeds, particularly effective in this domain, compete for first place in the hearts of woodcock hunters.

The Saint-Germain Hound is a half-blood, born from the crossbreeding between a pointer and a Continental European hound. It is a rather rare dog.

France. This dog became fast, fiery, and dynamic and more than ever, earned its nickname "half-blood." Since then, breeders knew how to reinstitute more moderation in crossbreedings, and the Saint-Germain Hound recovered a style and an appearance closer to the Hound.

But today, this dog may still be considered as a compromise between the Pointer and the Continental European hound. This hunting dog with a large nose has a sustained gait, tracks with its head high, and displays dominating points. It is a dog that hunts essentially in plains. However, it is more versatile than some people say. There are very few of these dogs; as a result, breeders of the Saint-

Germain Hound must often resort to pointers to avoid too much in-breeding. This produces dogs that are effective for sure, but today one may well wonder about the real temperament and style of the Saint-Germain Hound.

Other French Hounds

Due to the extremely localized nature of French dog breeding, breeds of hounds that certain regions developed for a long time have completely disappeared today. Some people try to re-create these breeds regularly. These people have various motives, from a desire to distinguish themselves by developing a breed to a real desire to preserve the heritage of their land. But it seems quite useless to want to re-create a breed that is already extinct, which is the case, for example, with the Ariège Hound.

This dog from the Pyrenees was certainly born of French Hounds and hounds from the Ariège region, from which this dog gets its lively temperament. At the beginning of the century the breed was very widespread in its region but today, it has totally disappeared. However, some people try to resurrect it based on personal testimonies and according to some illustrations. But it is rather presumptuous to think that this revival might produce a dog that would correspond to what the Ariège Hound once was.

The same can be said of the Dupuy Hound. For some, this dog was created from crossing a Sloughi (a Greyhound breed) with a French Hound. For others, it came from a cross between hounds from the Poitou region. What is certain is that its native region is Poitou. Today, this powerfully built dog might have disappeared.

British Pointers:
Speed and Specialization

Great Britain has very few breeds of pointers compared to France. This is a result of an evolution of hunting and breeding that is quite different from the one known in France. During the Revolution, the French acquired the right to hunt for everyone, which multiplied the number of hunters and consequently the number of regional breeds. During the same period, hunters from across the Channel experienced the exact opposite situation. On the British Isles, hunting had always been a privilege reserved to those who owned land. There was no revolution in Great Britain, thus, no redistribution of property: no "democratization" of hunting occurred. The persons who could hunt were rich—and this is still the case today.

Covering huge areas, the British practiced mainly three kinds of hunting: stag hunting (without dogs), fox hunting with hounds, and small upland game hunting with the assistance of spaniels, retrievers, or pointers. Hoping to develop breeds that would correspond to their different kinds of hunting, the hunters tended toward extreme specialization. At the same time, French popular hunters needed all-purpose dogs. Thus, while French hunters would praise only "all-around dogs," British hunters responded by choosing dogs adapted to each method of hunting.

Again, contrary to French hunters who appreciated hunting at random and variety of game, hunters from England specialized their pointers to hunt three kinds of upland game. In their opinion, the only birds worth hunting were grouses, young partridges, and snipes. They found it uninteresting and even humiliating to shoot any other pointed game. The grouse, young partridge, and snipe had a common characteristic: they lived in vast and totally open areas—large agricultural land in the case of the young partridge, heathland in the case of the grouse, and marshland in the case of the snipe. In these environments, there are neither hedgerows nor thickets. Therefore, hunters needed dogs that hunted quickly and far to explore these vast areas and to flush game. British pointers were always selected based on these two criteria. Moreover, they needed to have a powerful nose to be able to pick up the scent of game over large distances. One can readily see that these dogs were at the opposite spectrum of French hunters' tastes in dogs. French hunters were looking for versatile, not too fast, and methodical dogs, capable of hunting a multitude of game over extremely diverse areas. These differences between the British and the French still exist today.

Another very simple reason might explain why there are only four breeds of British pointers. British hunters, who were

The Irish Setter owes its success among nonhunters to its superb mahogany coat. But this dog is, above all, an extraordinary hunter.

necessarily wealthy and therefore few, were quick to practice selective breeding. These noblemen traveled a lot. At the mercy of invitations and courtesy calls, they crossed their dogs with other excellent quality dogs. As all found themselves at the home of Count or Duke So-and-So for going hunting, regional breeds were practically nonexistent. One could hardly talk about differences between different breeds. Besides, this selection was based on significant inbreeding that prevented the development of diverse breeds.

One must also take into account the interest that British people have in dog breeding. Very quickly, British people organized dogs shows and invented field trials. These events encouraged the mixing, selection, and finally the emergence of a small number of very well-selected breeds. In France at that time, the regional dog, even the district dog, was king. In addition, British breeds at first all had about the same colors, namely white with tan and black spots. The more pronounced differences in their coats are more recent.

In the field, hunters (sportsmen, as they called themselves) favored the specialization of their dogs to the utmost. Thus, it was at least improper to make the dog flush game in brushwoods, as well as make him retrieve game. The British used spaniels for flushing game from brushwoods, and retrievers for retrieving.

The hunter who hunted grouse in Scotland went over the sandy moor behind his pointers or his setters. He was escorted by a guard who carried the bagged game and kept the retriever specialized in retrieving. For the sportsman, this extreme specialization was synonymous with effectiveness and objectivity. It was this state of mind that presided over the development of British pointers.

The performance of these dogs attracted many European hunters, who started to import them. Year after year, breeding of these dogs increased in Continental Europe. French and Italian hunters modified their British dogs to render them a little more versatile. They knew how to maintain and even increase the effectiveness of their dogs while preserving the style of hunting inherent in each breed. From their point of view, the British were not able to import Continental European dogs. As hunting in Great Britain was the privilege of a small number of persons, selection in breeding was made using a lesser number of studs, so that today many hunters believe that British purebred dogs born in France or Italy are often better hunters than English dogs. Nevertheless, these tremendous hunting dogs, pointers and setters, are the fruit of the impassioned work of these astonishing

Previous page: A Gordon Setter retrieving a grouse in its native country, the Scottish moors. The work in these heathlands is not within the scope of all pointers.

A male and female English Setter, pointing a woodcock, with the dog behind respecting the other dog's point— a hunting action that all hunters worthy of the name dream about.

A great galloper, the Pointer is able to use its formidable effectiveness in woodcock hunting by moderating its gait, while maintaining the sweep of its quartering and the sharpness of its nose.

belonging to this or that sportsman. These sportsmen bred their dogs according to a very elaborate system of inbreeding. Although they used other breeds very little to improve their dogs, they often exchanged studs, so that a rather homogeneous single breed of pointers was rapidly born. Undisputed specialists of hunting over vast expanses, these dogs were destined to hunt young partridges and grouses.

Pointers, which arrived in France and other western European countries (Portugal, Germany, and Holland) during the nineteenth century, quickly became very successful among hunters who practiced their sport in the plains. They dominated setters in numbers until relatively recently.

The grand champion of springtime field trials, the pointer was for a long time feared by many Continental European hunters. "Too fast," "uncontrollable"—such were the most frequent criticisms of the Pointer. In fact, this reputation was not deserved. Although it is true that the Pointer walks quickly and far from its master, it is nevertheless one of the most exceptional hunting machines. Most of the time, it is a wonderful finder of game, endowed with an unrivaled nose and impressive physical abilities. It has a docile character and accepts training easily so long as the trainer does not try to make it a slow dog that hunts under the gun. Indeed, this dog is not fit for hunting pheasants in groups, but its skills made it accepted by plainsmen, woodcock hunters, snipe hunters, and mountain hunters. As a matter of fact, the Pointer's intelligence allows it to adjust to very different hunting practices as long as it is left with sufficient space to develop its quartering.

The only minor reproach of Pointers is that they tend to be either excellent or

sportsmen, to whom some of the most wonderful pointer breeds in the world owe their existence.

The Pointer

The Pointer is to pointers what the Ferrari is to cars. This dog represents the very essence of British pointers. However, its origins are rather Continental European because it was probably developed from Spanish Hounds which were brought back to Great Britain by noblemen hunters at the beginning of the eighteenth century. Originally, pedigree dogs became distinguishable as a result of different stud farms

Above: A superb Pointer in full action, showing the distinctive head carriage above the back line that allows it to catch the slightest scent carried by the wind even over a great distance.

Opposite: The point of the Pointer is impressive because this dog does not slow down when it catches the scent of game. From a full gallop, it drops into a point and holds staunchly like a statue in a dominant position that tends to make game freeze.

BRITISH POINTERS: SPEED AND SPECIALIZATION

Following page, top: The gallop
of the English Setter is lithe
and feline. It glides around
obstacles rather than noisily
trampling on brush, passing
over these obstacles with more
finesse than strength.

Bottom: The English Setter
points either lying down or in
a crouch. After catching the
scent of game, the dog draws
gradually closer to the ground
and ends by assuming this
typical position.

mediocre. Therefore, one should not hesitate, when purchasing a full-grown dog, to test its abilities before buying it.

The English Setter

In France, the English Setter is on the verge of overtaking the Brittany in number of births, which proves, better than any discourse, its effectiveness. Two men played an important role in the establishment of this breed. In the first half of the nineteenth century, Edward Laverack established the breed. Infatuated with dog shows, he made the English Setter a beautiful dog and a good hunter. Purcell Dewellin continued the work of his predecessor, but he gave greater emphasis to the dog's working qualities. The first of these two men opted for significant inbreeding and produced relatively heavy dogs. The latter resorted rather to new strengths with Irish and Scottish Setters and produced faster and smaller dogs. This duality is certainly the reason for the two distinct clubs in Great Britain. One gives preference to the beauty of the English Setter, while the other one prefers its working qualities, each club producing very different dogs.

In the United States and Canada, the English Setter was introduced at the end of the last century. Although it stayed in the shadow of the Pointer for a long time, the English Setter was able to show its ability and acquired a rising notoriety that is undeniable today. Its great intelligence allowed it to become the helper of many hunters who pursued quite different game. The English Setter's success also certainly lies in the dynamism of the English Setter Club and more particularly to its current president—J. M. Pilard, who contributed to bringing the breed to the highest steps of field trial podiums, while keeping the breed close to hunters' expectations.

The English Setter is certainly not a dog for everyone. Its origins make it best suited to hunters who operate alone or in small groups and who cover vast expanses where game is wild and difficult. It is only in such conditions that the English Setter can show its talents. Otherwise this dog

The English Setter is capable
of the finesse and prudence
needed when approaching and
pointing the lightest of game:
the marshland snipe that flys
away at the slightest warning.

only causes confusion in a line of hunters stalking pheasants or rabbits.

The English Setter has quite a particular style. Indeed, it hunts with effectiveness because of its ample quartering, speed, and powerful nose. But it is distinguished above all by its incomparable elegance. It has a feline posture and slithers over obstacles like a snake rather than overwhelm them with its strength. Its gallop is low to the ground. When it catches the scent of game, it crawls toward its prey like a deer. It points either crouching or lying down, which is always

The Irish wanted to produce a versatile Setter to hunt the great variety of game present on their island. They won the bet.

The Irish Setter

The Irish Setter has undoubtedly existed since the end of the seventeenth century in Ireland, but it was during the eighteenth century that people began talking about this dog. Originally, its coat could be of two colors: white with red spots, or red. Irish hunters developed a dog according to the constraints faced on their island. They had to deal with hard soil, often mountainous, sometimes marshy. Game was rare but also very diverse (grouses, woodcocks, pheasants, snipes, and ducks). Therefore, the Irish Setter was conceived first to be an enduring and persevering dog able to hunt for an entire day without seeing game. These two characteristics are still valid today. This dog was also more versatile than its British cousins.

Unfortunately, the Irish Setter quickly became the darling of nonhunters who liked the elegance of its flattering coat and its majestic head. Because of this, breeding quickly became based on aesthetic criteria.

On the British Isles, two quite different breeds could then be distinguished. One was tall and endowed with a superb coat of privileged beauty. The other one, selected for its working qualities, was shorter but more well balanced. Its usage was confidential. This distinction, which was very detrimental to the breed, was practiced in all countries. From then on, high-strung Setters were born with mediocre hunting qualities and doubtful psychic balance. Hunters realized this very quickly and gave this breed a disastrous reputation. However, some breeders continued to work. Their goal was to obtain a pure hunting dog. They succeeded in maintaining the primary

a surprise to those who do not know this kind of dog and expect it to perform a dominating point as the Pointer does. The Setter charms its victim, casts a spell over it and then serves it to the hunter on a platter. These talents make one forget easily about its disobedience. Indeed, the English Setter has but one fault that has discouraged more than one hunter: its inconstancy. It is as capricious as a movie star. With such a dog, the hunter does not have a helper but instead is the slave of his own capricious dog!

qualities of the "red devil" and soon the Irish Setter Club of America joined them. This club started a resolute policy of reestablishment so that the Setter could serve its main purpose: hunting.

One should also note the work done by exceptional breeders such as John Nash, who passed away in 1990, and who took the Red Setters to the highest steps of field trial podiums. Nash exported many dogs throughout Europe and contributed significantly to the reestablishment of the hunting Irish Setter.

Today there are several stocks of Irish Setters that generally produce good hunting dogs. With their good size, these dogs have a magnificent hunting style. Despite the fact that some woodcock hunters blame Irish Setters for the color of their coat, which makes them almost invisible in underbrush, these dogs can be murderous in hunting most small game. The amplitude of their quartering is equivalent to that of the English Setter.

In the United States, Canada, and various European countries, Irish Setters

After enduring the baneful effects of fashion, the Irish Setter made a noticeable comeback in field trials and hunting.

The Gordon Setter is the bulkiest setter. It is also certainly the most majestic setter and the one with the greatest endurance.

that hunt are still few despite of the efforts made by the various Irish Setter clubs. Show setters are quite different morphologically and are much more numerous. The hunter who wishes to purchase one of these dogs should be very careful when it comes to the choice of breeding. The best thing to do is to choose a breed that shows consistent results in springtime field trials instead of choosing only a champion stud

for breeding, because even a champion can produce undesirable offspring. There are also trainers who know this breed well and who can give useful advice to a hunter who wishes to find an Irish Setter.

The Gordon Setter

The Gordon Setter descended from the selection made by the Duke of Gordon in his Scottish castle. For this reason, this dog is sometimes also called a Scottish Setter.

In the eighteenth century, Gordon, who was an impenitent hunter, noticed that English Setters, except the larger ones, were not perfectly adjusted to grouse hunting in the difficult Scottish moors where the terrain and the climate were often too hard for these dogs. Gordon thus chose to cross English Setters with sheepdogs from the region that often had a black coat, which is why Gordon Setters were black, tan, and white. This crossbreeding also explains their endurance and rusticity.

The Gordon Setter is the heaviest of British dogs. Its hunting style is quite different from the other Anglo-Saxon breeds. Some people say that it is the most Continental European of British dogs. Indeed, the Gordon hunts less quickly than the English or Irish Setter. It alternately trots and gallops, in the same way as many Continental European dogs.

The dog is methodical and scours the terrain while always staying close to its master. While other setters show ardor and passion, the Gordon shows prudence and moderation. It has infallible endurance. The Gordon's characteristics make it a perfect helper for woodcock hunting, in spite of the black-and-tan (and occasionally black, white, and tan) coat that make it barely visible in dark undergrowth.

Although the Gordon Setter has many good qualities, it never achieved huge success with European and American hunters. This lack of interest might be due to the dog's lack of style. It is much less spectacular in action than the other British dogs. To a lesser extent, one must also recognize that the Gordon Setter suffers from the same ills as the Irish Setter: a considerable part of the stock is devoted to shows and the Gordon's working qualities are thus neglected.

Although the Gordon does not have the vigor of Irish and English setters, it is nevertheless a quality dog. It hunts like a British dog—that is, far from its master, so it is not recommended for those sportsmen who hunt game in groups.

Whereas all other English pointers hunt at a gallop, the Gordon alternates a surging gallop with a brisk trot. Not as fast as British pointers, it takes more after a marathon runner than a sprinter.

German Pointers:
Rigor and Versatility

To have a good understanding of what German Pointers are, one must take a close look at the way German hunters use dogs in their sport. Big-game hunting in Germany has always been more important than small-game hunting. German hunters are the greatest specialists of stalking deer and wild boar. They are also very fond of big-game battue and respect the very strict limits on the number of animals that may be killed each season. But for all that, small game is not neglected.

Hunting is a serious matter in Germany. German hunting laws make game crop products, like woods or farmland. Thus, the question is how to manage and increase these assets. From this approach to hunting, different breeds of pointers developed.

First and foremost, the German hunter is the manager of a hunting territory with which he is entrusted for a specific amount of time. He has the mission not only to maintain this territory but also to make it profitable. In Germany, there is no collective hunting on common land. Most of the time, hunting territories belong to parishes that rent them by auction to one individual or to a very small group of hunters. This lease may be terminated at any time if the management of the terrain is considered defective. This system of land management is very old.

The German hunter practices several methods of hunting on the territory that he has leased. He silently stalks yearling roe-bucks and wild boars and shoots them. He also assures the regulation of harmful animals, shoots a few partridges and pheasants, rolls a hare once in a while, and shoots passing ducks. Moreover, he does the work of a gamekeeper (sharing land, trapping, policing hunts, etc.)

The German hunter's dog follows its master in all his activities. The dog has to walk calmly and quietly at its master's side. It must fetch, even rip the throat out of large wounded game, or flush a hare or a wild boar with its bark. It has to point a pheasant, retrieve it, or find a wounded bird. It should also be able to kill harmful animals and even attack a poacher!

This great versatility is sanctioned by a very thorough and serious field-trial competition called V.G.P. (which is the abbreviation of a German term) in which the perfectly trained dog must show all its talents. Could the German Pointer be the archetype of the perfect dog, capable of replacing a hound, a pointer, a spaniel, a retriever, a bloodhound, and even a watchdog? Obviously, that is what certain hunters think when they import German dogs at great cost.

However, it is necessary to modify this overly enthusiastic portrait. German Pointers are certainly the most versatile of

German hunters make their dogs take numerous qualifying working tests quite different from those in other countries.

all dogs. But by wanting to be good in everything, they are often average in everything they do. Moreover, although the V.G.P. is a very complete trial, it really just shows the tremendous capacity of the dog to accept training, surely the main quality of German dogs. Once this test is passed, hunters specialize their companions in a more precise field according to their needs. Obviously, rare are the dogs that will have the opportunity to practice all the disciplines for which they have been trained.

A French hunter attending a German field trial held in a plain would surely find German dogs much less talented than French Pointers. This is the price of being versatile. Nevertheless, German Pointers correspond perfectly to German hunters' expectations.

However, the use of German breeds in other countries is quite different. One can say without mistake that German pointers produced in America, Canada, England, and France are largely superior to their counterparts for hunting truly wild upland game. French hunters, for example, were able to use the extraordinary ability for training that German dogs have. Deliberately, French hunters succeeded in adjusting them to their own hunting habits, and were able to change these dogs into diabolical hunting machines that are versatile to be sure, but only intended for small game.

The method of training called the "German way" is very strict. It is well suited to a certain type of hunter who does not want to be burdened with the moods of British dogs (how easy to understand them!), but who wish to own dogs that are more modern than other sporting breeds. In fact, the creation of German Pointers is relatively recent. Indeed, they have a faster hunting speed

The German hunter is a solitary hunter who hunts small and big game alike. His dog must be able to do the same.

and a nose that is often superior to other Continental European breeds. Because of these traits, they represent a good compromise between British dogs and other Continental European dogs. Their ability to hunt big game and harmful animals has more or less disappeared, but can still be developed with the help of training based on great obedience and in which the hunter shows firm authority.

To sum up, British dogs are artists full of initiative, French dogs are shrewd hunters, and German dogs are the elite troops! It is still important to point out that in many European countries, as well as in America and Canada, hunters greatly

This German Pointer, assuredly pointing gray partridges in a field of stubble, perfectly illustrates the use of German breeds by French hunters.

Following page: This big German Pointer retrieving a fox epitomizes the German use of this breed. These two dogs illustrate very well the enormous difference in how pointers are conceived of on each side of the Rhine River— versatility versus specialization.

transformed German dogs to make them more suitable to their hunting practices. Today, these dogs are consequently very different from the German conception. German hunters would have difficulty recognizing their own dogs among German Pointers and French Drahthaars. British dogs themselves, which also had to adjust to the Continental hunters' needs remain considerably closer to the British

conception, whereas German breeds raised in for example France became quasi-French breeds.

The German Shorthaired Pointer or German Pointer

The German Shorthaired Pointer is the most widespread pointer in the world. In many European countries, as well as in the United States and Canada, it holds a special place in hunters' hearts, and it establishes itself among the most frequently used hunting companions. In field trials, it is the only rival to the Brittany.

The German Shorthaired Pointer, a relatively recent breed whose origin goes back to the middle of the last century, was able to adjust to the modern hunting conditions, just as the Brittany did. If, in Germany, its versatility is carefully preserved, anywhere else, he is considered as a pure pointer.

The German Shorthaired Pointer is a fast dog with ample quartering, capable of hunting the most difficult game. The power of its nose loses nothing by comparison with the nose of any of the British galloping dogs.

Very intelligent, this dog knows how to adjust to every hunting condition and shows a rare ability when trained. But some hunters find it a bit difficult. One might occasionally hear a hunter mutter, "You have to strike a hound." Certainly, training a German Shorthaired Pointer demands great firmness because this dog has the annoying habit of compelling its master to recognize its worth. But firmness does not mean violence! The German Shorthaired Pointer's training is also facilitated by its great candor. It is not capricious like a "diva," which would require the talents of a canine psychologist.

This German Shorthaired Pointer retrieving a gray partridge clearly shows a very soft mouth. This is a quality that German dogs sometimes unfortunately lack.

Although retrieving is always very easy to achieve with these dogs, some German Shorthaired Pointers have rough teeth. This unfortunate trait is undoubtedly the result of the process of eliminating harmful animals that was imposed on these dogs in Germany. Even more serious is the fact that certain breeders misused the Pointer's blood to obtain a faster dog able to win in the field trials. Certainly, this is true of only a small number of dog breeders, but it is advisable to be careful when choosing a dog in order to avoid finding oneself with a brown Pointer! One should notice that although German Pointers are typically brown and white, very often there are certain subjects with the prevailing color of black which have the same abilities.

The German Wirehaired Pointer or Drahthaar

At the end of the last century, German breeders could no longer bear to see English dogs invading Continental Europe. Thus they decided to create an ideal dog, capable of responding to every hunter's expectations and able to supplant the other breeds. Thanks to a clever cocktail of breeds (Hound, Pointer, Poodle, Terrier, etc.), they developed the Drahthaar. After certain difficulties in stabilizing the breed, they obtained this hound gifted with very particular hair called wire (*Draht* in German) that corresponds perfectly to the Germanic concept of hunting dogs. The Drahthaar was supposed to do everything: a retriever that likes water and is aggressive toward big game. It is also a bloodhound that points and kills harmful animals. The versatile abilities of this dog are attracting many of today's hunters.

However, it is a good idea to be careful. To be sure, the Wirehaired

All German Pointers have remarkable abilities and the mind of a hunter.

Some German Shorthaired Pointers became famous in the green crops of springtime fields by outperforming Brittanies, which were favored. This shows also the great adaptability of this breed, which can shine in a discipline for which it was not originally intended. In other respects, the ability of this dog to lay a deer out after tracking its blood trail demands the kind of energy that few breeds have. However, one might have two small misgivings concerning this breed.

Pointer sometimes makes an excellent pointer, but some of them do not master this discipline well. Training them also demands a strong grip on the hunter's part. One should be aware that the Wirehaired Pointer shows immoderate fondness for big game, and does not always resist the temptation of chasing a deer or a wild boar, which might be awkward for a small game hunter.

On the other hand, the hunter who, like his German counterparts, wishes to have an all-purpose dog will find a perfect helper in this breed. But the Wirehaired

Above: The Wirehaired Pointer, considered the champion of versatility by German hunters, shows itself to be a very honest marshland retriever.

Opposite: The Wirehaired Pointer, here pointing, has recently attracted many American and European hunters. Its coat may be brown and white or black and white.

Above: The Weimaraner is an aristocrat among German dogs. In the past, prospective owners were required to have at least three degrees of nobility to be able to purchase one of these dogs.

Right: There is an almost unknown variety of longhaired Weimaraner, but they are rarely seen hunting.

Pointer is far from having fulfilled the ambition of his creators.

The hunter hunting at random who would choose this type of dog runs a big risk of finding himself with a helper that is totally unsuited to his method of hunting.

The Weimaraner

In the past, the Weimaraner was reserved for German nobility. It is a very ancient breed that suffered from its aristocratic use. In fact, three degrees of nobility were necessary to enjoy the privilege of owning a Weimaraner! After World War II, the breed was saved from extinction by

American soldiers, who were attracted by his inimitable color. Nowadays, its great elegance confines it principally to the role of companion. Indeed, the Weimaraner Club tries by all means to preserve the breed's hunting abilities, but there is no denying that the number of subjects in the field is extremely low.

With few exceptions, on the hunt the Weimaraner has a well-balanced, short quartering, which is not to say slow, but does not have an exceptional nose. This dog is relatively easy to train. The hunter who is eager to enlist the services of a brilliant helper would do better by directing his attention toward another breed, unless being noticed in the street with such a beautiful dog is what really matters to him. We should also mention the existence of a variety of longhaired Weimaraner, whose abilities are even more doubtful.

The Langhaar

For many people, the Langhaar is a kind of German Pointer with long hair. This is a serious mistake: this dog is, in fact, a spaniel. Its big size and style might be explained by the frequent crosses of this breed with Irish and Gordon Setters.

However, the Langhaar hunts like a Continental European dog. It has the most adaptable character of all dogs of Germanic origin.

The Langhaar is rarely seen in the United States and Canada, just as in Germany and France where few exist. On the other hand, in the Netherlands there are very beautiful Langhaars that shine regularly in international competitions. The Langhaar, gifted with an active and ample quartering, surely deserves to be more successful. A hunter who makes the

Contrary to appearance, the Langhaar is not a longhaired German hound. It is rather closer to spaniels by its history and its character

effort to go to the Netherlands will have surely the good fortune of joining up with a helper that is rigorous but easy to train.

The Pudelpointer

In the middle of the last century, a few German dog breeders, envious of the Pointer's performance but aware of this dog's limitations, decided to create a wire-haired pointer better suited to their methods of hunting.

They crossed the Poodle and the Pointer, knowing that crossing shorthaired and curly-haired dogs produces wire-haired dogs. In addition, the dog they sought to create had to have the nose, quartering, and passion of the Pointer, but also the fondness for water, the hatred for harmful animals, and the intelligence of the Poodle. Although very appealing, this goal is only a dream.

After a few generations, dogs created from this type of crossbreeding always end up reverting to the specific type of one of the breeds used to produce the new breed. Under the circumstances, because the Pointer's contribution was the preponderant strain, Pudelpointers rapidly became Pointers with a more or less wire-haired coat.

Even today, the breed continues to try to define itself and breeders have difficulties in stabilizing it. Indeed, the Pudelpointer has suffered from competing with the Wirehaired Pointers, which had much more success.

Breeders were never really interested in the Pudelpointer and their numbers are less than weak on both sides of the Rhine River.

The Münster Spaniel or Münsterlander

The Münster Spaniel (or Münsterlander) is to Germany what the Brittany is to France. This breed includes two varieties: one, which is the size of a hound, is not very widespread even in its country of origin; the other, which is smaller, barely taller than the Brittany, is clearly more common.

As its name suggests, the Pudelpointer is a dog that derives both from Continental European breeds and the Pointer. It has never met with success.

The Münsterlander, selected from longhaired and shorthaired dogs, is—like all German pointers—able to hunt large as well as small game. However, its abilities as a pointer are prevailing, which make the Münster Spaniel a very decent wood and marshland dog. Its point is very firm and its nose is sure and powerful.

The Münster Spaniel shows great vitality. This last characteristic, however, does not make training difficult because this dog is an exceptionally accommodating helper. True and straightforward, this dog does not try to deceive its master.

This hunting dog does have its limitations, however. A little short in its quartering, this dog is not well suited for hunting in plains.

In many European countries its numbers are consistently on the rise, which proves that European hunters recognize this animal as an extremely useful companion. Their only reservation is that the Münster Spaniel tends to hunt deer rather than woodcock, when this larger game is present.

The Small Münsterlander, which is more widespread than the Large Münsterlander, is a good compromise between German and French dogs.

Other Pointers

The Wirehaired Pointing Griffon or Korthals Griffon is neither completely French, nor completely German, nor completely Dutch; it is a real European!

Apart from French, British and German pointers, there are other breeds of pointers in various European countries worthy of mention. Most of the time, these dogs remained rather close to their initial Continental European type: relatively heavy dogs with rather circumscribed and slow quartering.

Although these breeds are not always well represented in the United States, Canada, and Europe, they are sometimes very common in the hunting fields of their native country. Nevertheless, these breeds suffer from merciless competition from foreign breeds that are more modern and more numerous. Thus, in Italy, Italian Hounds and Spinoni are well represented but are significantly outnumbered by setters and pointers, whose abilities attracted transalpine hunters.

On the other hand, in Hungary, the Vizsla is still the most prevalent pointer. It is also interesting to note that many of these breeds were used in the development of more recent breeds, such as the hounds from the Iberian Peninsula, which were the origin of pointers. However, hunters today are flocking in great numbers to faster breeds that have a more powerful nose and wider quartering. The survival of certain old European breeds, which played such an important part in the history of hunting, seems to be in jeopardy.

The Italian Hound

This massive dog, with slightly drooping features and an impressive frame, is a very ancient breed that has hardly changed during the course of its history. It is certainly one of the very first breeds of pointers to have been established. In France as well as in Italy, this breed can be seen in many paintings dating from the Renaissance.

Although the Italian Hound came very close to extinction, in the 1970s it again found a fairly considerable number of followers from the other side of the Alps. These people succeeded in preserving its inimitable style. Indeed, the Bracco trots at an amble, that is it always raises first both legs on one side, then both on the other. For it, galloping is considered as a mistake. But it is not always easy to keep this dog trotting when one realizes how important crossing this dog with the pointer was in the past. Although this breed might appear as little more than a curiosity, the

The Italian Hound—heir to the great tradition of Italian dog lovers from the Renaissance.

Perfectly adapted to hunting in the thickets of southern Europe, the Italian Spinoni did not meet with the success that it deserves with hunters in the south of France.

number of births registered each year in Italy is impressive. The absence of the Italian Hound in France might be explained by the fact that it does not possess any qualities that local breeds do not already have, such as the Blue Auvergne Hound or the French Gascony Hound. In the field, the Italian Hound shows a relatively sharp nose. It is a calm dog, easy to train, but with a rather slow gait. It always hunts close to its master.

The Spinoni

At the beginning of the century, when every breed was indiscriminately crossed with British breeds, the Spinoni, this solid

Continental European Griffon, resisted the trend. It is surely one of the very rare Continental breeds that was not mixed with pointer or setter blood. All credit belongs to Italian dog lovers who have bequeathed to us a Griffon true to its original type. This big dog is characterized by its almost entirely white coat. The presence of brown reveals a "shameful" union with the Korthals Griffon. The Spinoni hunts at a trot and never strays from the hunter. It covers terrain at its own pace and methodically rakes it. Try as you might to tire it, you will be exhausted before this dog is. It displays extraordinary endurance and is not afraid of cold, rain, heat, or the thickest vegetation. Rocky landscapes with sparse vegetation, such as the sun-drenched hills in Mediterranean regions, are its favorite terrain. The Spinoni has a few shortcomings: a slightly short nose and a tendency to transform itself into a hound. To find a breeder that offers a satisfactory selection, you have to go to Italy.

The Hungarian Pointer or Vizsla

The Hungarian Pointer, which is characterized by its fawn-colored coat, has a very ancient origin. The Hungarians were able to rapidly develop their own breed of pointer. However, the numbers of the Vizsla (the other name of the Hungarian Pointer) were always low because possession of this dog was reserved for the nobility. Not until the middle of the last century did this dog become widespread throughout its native country. The first Vizslas were imported in the United States in the 1950s, and the breed was admitted to AKC registry in 1960.

In fact, there are two Hungarian Pointers. The first one is shorthaired and is a cousin of the German Pointer because of numerous crosses between the two breeds. The similarities of behavior between these two dogs are disconcerting, but they are both different. The Hungarian Pointer does not hunt as rapidly or as far away as its German cousin. Easier to manage than the German Pointer, training it does not require as much firmness. On the other hand, its sense of smell is often slightly weaker.

The second Hungarian Pointer is a recent creation, dating from between the two world wars. Morphologically, it looks like the first one, but has a very rough, wirehaired coat. What the first Hungarian Hound owes to the German Pointer, the second owes to the Drahthaar. Its coat makes it fit to hunt in difficult terrains.

This dog might be an interesting dog for the hunter who likes German Pointers but who wishes to have a more easygoing companion. One should be cautious, however, because certain lines are frequently gun-shy. Thus, the hunter must be especially careful when choosing his dog.

The Korthals Griffon or Wirehaired Pointing Griffon

It is difficult to classify the Korthals Griffon among the dogs of a particular country. Without a doubt, it was the only truly European dog before its time! At least it should be judged as such. Edward Karel Korthals was a Dutch gamekeeper stationed in German territory. In the middle of the last century, he decided to create a breed of Pointing Griffon that would be versatile and unmistakably Continental. He

The Hungarian Pointer is very popular with hunting guides in its native country. These are a shorthaired and a wirehaired variety.

then used several breeds of diverse origins—Dutch, French, Belgian, and German dogs. In his kennels, he had several hundred subjects, from which he made his rigorous selection. At the end of his life, his bet paid off. The Korthals Griffon was born and the breed was firmly established.

What characterizes the Korthals above all is its inimitable snout, composed of a mustache and bushy eyebrows. Under its wiry hair, which resembles the bristles of a wild boar, there is a downy undercoat. This coat gives the Korthals a very rustic look. This dog can adjust to any climate or environment: it is impervious to the cold, rain, snow, and ice.

Indeed, it is a rustic dog, but not devoid of passion. When the Korthals Griffon usually hunts at a trot, it is also able to alternate this pace with a feline and dynamic gallop. This Griffon has never been and will never be a dog for field trials. It is, above all, a dog for practical hunting. Easy to train, the Korthals is suitable for a hunter who does not wish to have a dog that is too touchy. It is an excellent retriever and hunts pheasant as well as woodcock and snipe.

As for its defects, one might mention a certain fondness for large game and a quartering that is sometimes too narrow. Also worth recalling is that some Korthals Griffons have too much English blood to be able to win field trials. Faster than their brethren, they are easily recognizable by their slender appearance and lack of an undercoat—indisputable proof that the dog has a pointer as a close ancestor.

Today, the Korthals Griffon is indisputably a "French" dog, even though it was born in Germany of European parents under the guiding hand of a Dutch master. It is in France that almost all these dogs and the best subjects are found.

In the United States the breed is well established and particularly adapted for swampy country. The Wirehaired Pointing Griffon is a strong swimmer and has a catlike gracefulness.

A few relics

Besides the breeds previously mentioned, in Europe and especially in the Iberian Peninsula, there are a few other breeds worth mentioning that are extremely scarce. In Portugal, the Perdiguero is a relatively bulky hound that is certainly the origin of the pointer. In Spain, the Burgos hound is a heavy dog that looks a little like an Italian Hound. This breed is in the process of dying out. We should also mention the Czech Bearded Dog, which in fact is only a descendant of the Stichelhaar, the old German Pointing Griffon that has practically disappeared today.

Previous page: After having been a huge success among French hunters, today the Korthals Griffon seems to be marking time. Competition with the Drahthaar has certainly contributed to this fact.

Particularly fit for hunting woodcock, the Korthals Griffon is very much liked by lovers of this game.

Retrievers

Retrievers: Retrieving First

Among hunting dogs, there is one category that stands apart that is underestimated by many: retrievers. As we saw previously, English pointers, such as setters and pointers, are specialists, as opposed to Continental European pointers that are more generalist. Their aim is to find upland game alive and to point it. It thus became necessary to have a helper solely fit for retrieving shot game. Indeed, English hunters developed retrievers to avoid making their pointers retrieve.

The role of retrievers is very simple. They must be able to follow the pointer at a respectable distance to avoid disturbing it. When the setter points, the retriever must respect the other dog's point, that is, stop automatically or sit. Then, it must stay staunch when the game takes flight to allow the hunter to shoot. Once its master gives the command, the dog must fetch the game after having marked by sight where the game fell. If it is unable to visualize where the game fell, the dog's nose must follow the eyes and it should be able to find the wounded bird after persistent tracking. It must then return to the hunter as quickly as possible and put the game in its master's hand.

Anglo-Saxon hunters perfected the work of retrievers by teaching them retrieving exclusively. During a battue hunt or when hunting ducks from a blind, the dog must sit staunch at the feet of the shooter while memorizing the points where different birds fell. Then, on command, it must fetch and retrieve the different game, without forgetting any. Every breed of British retrievers was produced with this goal in mind, and they are used in this way in their native country.

Not all retrievers come from the British Isles. There are also two breeds native to North America that are intended exclusively for waterfowl game. These dogs are rather close to British retrievers, which is not surprising, since nearly all British retrievers have an ancestor that originated from the cold regions of North American.

Certain Continental European breeds are also classified in the retriever category. These dogs were selected to produce breeds intended for retrieving waterfowl. These helpers had a coat perfectly suitable for water and had a great sense for retrieving. Like pointers, Continental water dogs first had to be all-around dogs able to perform several different tasks. Thus, the water dog had to be able to make a teal in a pond break cover, to retrieve a goose from deep water, and to flush a rabbit from thickets along marshes. Indeed, in the way they hunt, these dogs were more closely connected to spaniels that do not point than real retrievers.

The best known of these breeds, the Poodle, has completely disappeared today from hunting fields. It is truly difficult to believe that this sweet dog used to be a fearless waterfowl dog, not so long ago. Still, most Continental European water breeds descend from the Poodle. Its presence can be found in the origins of famous hunting dogs: the Drahthaar, Pudelpointer, and the Irish Water Spaniel. Sadly, the Poodle is no longer used by hunters specializing in waterfowl nor is it classified as a hunting

dog even though certain breeds, which really should be categorized as companion dogs, are still classified as hunting dogs.

There are other dogs that are not classified in the categories that correspond to the type of work they do. This is the case for the Irish Water Spaniel. Although it is grouped with spaniels, it looks like Continental water dogs in all respects and does the same kind of work.

As one can see, the category of retrievers covers dogs that are very different from each other, but, as their name suggests, all of them are helpers created for retrieving. Thus, they are specialized dogs.

A magnificent image of a Labrador at work, as all owners of this extraordinary dog should see him. Unfortunately, reality is often quite different.

Previous page: Originally from Canada, retrievers are perfect for hunting the many waterfowls of the wide North American continent. A beaver dam is an excellent hiding place!

The Labrador Retriever

The most widespread of retrievers and one of the most recent, the Labrador as we know him today appeared in the last century. To be sure, this dog, which originated in the northern part of New Quebec, had been present in Great Britain as early as the eighteenth century, but British hunters became interested in this dog only much later. Crossbreeding him with diverse breeds, especially with the Pointer, reduced the weight of this very heavy dog and developed his sense for hunting, without corrupting his innate taste for retrieving.

Numerous books deal with the Labrador's origins. Some mention the existence of a hypothetical dog that the fishermen of Newfoundland allegedly used to retrieve cod that escaped from the fishermen's nets. This is a nice story but is hardly plausible, considering that a day fishing for cod is spent in frigid weather where the seas often run high. What is sure is that this dog is exceedingly fond of water. Its tail, which is used like a rudder, is slightly reminiscent of an otter's tail. In addition, there is also a legend about a crossbreed between this small mammal and a dog!

Every dog has developed membranes between their toes, but the membrane of the Labrador is especially well developed. Some people even say that it has webbed paws. This is certainly an overstatement, but this unusual feature certainly allows Labradors to swim easily. Its dense and oily coat is also well suited to water.

What must be emphasized above all with the Labrador are its extraordinary hunting qualities, which are achieved due to the selective breeding by British and American breeders. The Labrador has an

The Labrador will always be far superior to all the other breeds of hunting dogs in retrieving waterfowl so long as its origins and its training are irreproachable.

Following page, above: Calm and thoughtful, the Labrador does not hurry when it retrieves. It proceeds methodically and as a rule it should not forget a single wounded duck that has taken refuge on the shores of the pond.

Bottom: At ease on the ground as well as in the water, this Golden Retriever and Labrador illustrate well the versatility and effectiveness of retrievers when they retrieve game.

incredibly powerful nose that allows it to detect the fleeting scent of a wounded snipe, even from very far away. Tenacious, sometimes stubborn, the Labrador is able to fetch a winged bird, without any respite. The other great strength of this dog, which may be its greatest asset, is its visual memory. On this point, no other breed can compete. During a battue hunt, a Labrador is able to memorize the different drop spots of each bird shot, and can remember these spots to fetch the birds much later, without forgetting a single one. Endowed with a very "British" stolidness, it knows

how to be patient and can sit staunch at the hunter's side until given the retrieving command. Working both furry game as well as upland game, the Labrador is an exceptional hunting dog...in theory, unfortunately. Today, this enthusiastic picture must be slightly modified.

Who does *not* know what a Labrador is? For ten or twelve years, this dog has had such success with the public in general that everybody wants to have a Lab on a leash. It is the almost indispensable dog to stroll about in the beautiful neighborhoods of Paris, Berlin, Boston, or Ottawa. This fashion continues unabated, and owners of Labradors are becoming more and more numerous. To satisfy this demand, breeders who are not very scrupulous have neglected all principles of selective breeding. More serious still, the Retriever Club of France for example, encouraged the emergence of a stock founded only on esthetic criteria and not on the characteristics of an efficient hunting dog. The truth must be faced:

"beauty" champions at dog shows from the end of the 1980s through the beginning of the 1990s were, with a few rare exceptions, totally unsuited for hunting work.

Today, the trend seems to be reversed, but is it not too late? The Labrador is an example of the destruction of a working breed, sacrificed on the altar of fashion. These dogs became aggressive, hypernervous, and uncontrollable. Some even refuse to jump into the water. What hunter has not witnessed this sad spectacle of this once-noble breed's degradation? Certainly, there are still serious breeders who produce excellent working dogs, but they are rare. The hunter who wishes to buy a Labrador must be very cautious.

The Golden Retriever

For many people, the Golden Retriever is a longhaired Labrador. "Absolutely not!" fans of this breed retort. Indeed, the Golden Retriever is very different from its cousin, the Labrador, in its physical appearance, as well as in its hunting style. The Golden Retriever is more slender, has a thinner head, and a golden coat that varies from a sandy color to a profound gold, whereas the Labrador's coat may be gold, black, or brown.

All the same, popular beliefs often contain a basic truth, and the current resemblance between the Golden Retriever and the Labrador is enough to make one wonder. Indeed, it is difficult not to speculate that the lack of Golden Retrievers prompted many breeders to crossbreed the two clandestinely, gradually reducing the differences between the two breeds. But the Golden Retriever remains a very particular dog, with a very elegant longhaired coat.

A magnificent male Golden Retriever retrieving a pintail duck, which is also superb. Calmness is not a trait belonging exclusively to the Labrador.

The vogue that seized the Labrador benefited the Golden Retriever, which Europeans have discovered more recently. In the United States, the Golden Retriever is a very widespread companion dog.

Tired of seeing a dog once again corrupted by breeders, hunters are reluctant to choose him and few do. The same ills that plague the Labrador can be found accentuated in the Golden Retriever. Nevertheless, the Golden Retriever is fundamentally a hunting dog fit for retrieving waterfowl. Its style, which is different from the Labrador's, is faster but also more irregular. Its sense of smell is excellent and makes for good tracking and game finding.

The Flat-Coated Retriever

Flat-Coated Retrievers are rather popular in the United States and Canada as well as in their native country (Great Britain), although not as popular as the Labrador and the Golden Retriever, which are well known for their more acute nose. The Flat-Coated Retriever, a more ancient retriever with an aristocratic appearance, might have been born from crossing Newfoundlands, Irish Setters, and retrievers, which gives it great performing speed in the field. The Flat-Coat is unafraid of cold water and thick coverts, is highly intelligent and

Though it may greatly resemble the Labrador, the Golden Retriever displays a very different style of hunting—more energetic but less methodical.

The Flat-Coated Retriever has a thinner appearance than other retrievers. Setter's blood runs in its veins.

companionable, and remains playful for many years. Training demands a certain skill and a lot of patience because it is very sensitive and not a fast learner.

But the Flat-Coat has one advantage over the other retrievers: fashion, hence commercial breeders, has not touched him yet. The purchase of a good-quality puppy with all the natural working abilities is still possible. In Great Britain, its native country, the Flat-Coat is part of hunting history, and its name can be found in many books. Its straight and flat-lying coat is black, sometimes liver, of moderate length, density, and fullnes, with a high luster.

The Curly-Coated Retriever

The fourth and last retriever of British origin, the Curly-Coated Retriever has the most astonishing appearance. Its curly short-haired coat gives it a unique appearance, similar to that of Continental European water dogs from the beginning of this century, such as the Poodle. It is also the tallest of the retrievers. In its native country, the Curly-Coat enjoyed considerable success as a companion dog in the middle of the last century. Previously, it was used for hunting waterfowl, as were most curly-haired dogs from the beginning

of this century. Today, its numbers have dwindled everywhere. Thus, it seems inevitable that serious selective breeding based on working qualities will be compromised by the absence of available sires.

The Curly-Coat is said to be calm and steady, but training it demands patience and skill. It is a performing hunting dog but is slow to show its true potential. As the oldest retriever breed—descending from the 16th century English Water Spaniel—the Curly-Coat is especially part of the history of dog lovers and anyone who prizes originality will be drawn toward this breed.

The Chesapeake Bay Retriever

Although the Chesapeake Bay Retriever belongs to the family of British retrievers, it is quite different from them. This quiet breed developed in North America, on the Northeast Coast, as a helper for professional hunters of waterfowl, who hunted in order to live, no matter what the weather conditions were. It is a hard worker, with good endurance and also a good guard dog. Professional hunters often trusted it to keep their spoils when they were out celebrating after a day of

The Curly-Coated Retriever enjoyed considerable success in Great Britain during the last century as a companion dog more than as a hunting dog. Today, its numbers are dwindling.

Retriever has a role to play among waterfowlers, as the breed distinguishes itself through very independent work.

The Nova Scotia Duck-Tolling Retriever

Night falls on the marshland. After a day of repose, ducks prepare themselves to scatter into the night, searching for food. Very curious, the ducks have all noticed the fox that is trotting along the bank. Knowing that they are safe in the water, the ducks go toward the predator to see it more closely. Imperceptibly, pressed close together, they get closer to the fox, while keeping a safe distance to assure their safety. That is what ducks do. They are truly the "caretakers" of the feathered tribe. Suddenly, like a thunderstorm, the blast of a shotgun can be heard. The birds fly away, flapping their wings. A second shot rings out. On the water, six ducks float, lifeless. A man comes out of the vegetation and whistles. The fox, which is none other than a dog, returns to the hunter, retrieving the first kill to him. The other five ducks will follow. This scene could have occurred in Canada, during the first half of the twentieth century in the province of Nova Scotia. Local hunters had noticed how curious ducks are and how they watch foxes, which thus gave them the idea of creating a breed that would look like a fox. Their goal was to make ducks gather together so they could be shot with a single blast of a shotgun. This practice also exists in other countries. The Nova Scotia Duck-Tolling Retriever, the smallest of retrievers, was born. Today this nice retriever, very different from other retrievers, is rapidly gaining popularity in Canada and the United States. Its

The Chesapeake Bay Retriever, very widespread in Canada and in the United States, is rare in Europe. It has never been a companion dog because of its rugged character.

hard work. The result was guaranteed! Nobody could get close to the game under the guard of such a watchdog! Very close to its origins, the Chesapeake Bay Retriever, or Chessie, as it is known in the United States, is a rough and rustic dog, good-natured and tolerant toward children. Although it is rather rare in Europe, many North American hunters use it because its work in marshland is exceptionally steady and efficient. Without a doubt, the Chesapeake Bay

resemblance to the fox, whose roguishness and slyness it also shares, is striking. It is difficult to discipline this dog, although it is quick to learn and highly intelligent. Although rather playful, this young breed, in terms of its willingness to work, is in no way inferior to the other breeds as a competent, eager-to-fetch hunting dog.

The Nova Scotia Duck-Tolling Retriever has a coat that is fairly long, sleek, and soft, with a dense, soft, waterproof undercoat. The dog is red or fawn—lighter than the Irish Setter. As stated, this dog is an excellent swimmer with outstanding endurance. In addition, the Nova Scotia Duck-Tolling Retriever is a notable guard dog.

A real curiosity, the Nova Scotia Duck-Tolling Retriever represents an anecdotal breed among the retriever family.

Retrievers in France: Specialists or Good All-Purpose Dogs?

The presence of retrievers in France, which is relatively ancient, experienced a resurgence at the beginning of the twentieth century. But for a long time, the use of these dogs was very discreet. At the time, owners of retrievers, who were often wealthy people, practiced battue hunting of small game. They could be seen especially in Sologne, Alsace, or in Ile-de-France. They used their dogs in a very conventional way, that is, only for retrieving. Most often, they hunted "the British way," with the retriever following its master and obeying him without being on a leash. Only a few hunters from the north of France, who frequently owned

British dogs, were the exceptions by hunting waterfowl.

This situation lasted until the end of the 1970s when retrievers, especially Labradors, became popular among hunters and nonhunters in a big way. There are various reasons for the success of this dog. Certainly, the presence of Labradors by the sides of statesmen like Valery Giscard d'Estaing, François Mitterand, and Jacques Chirac contributed to the popularity of this breed. Television also played a role. Advertisers regularly become infatuated with a dog breed and use it to promote all kinds of products. That was the case with the Labrador during the 1980s, so that many French people wanted to have this dog, among which were hunters.

That is how the Labrador made a noticeable appearance in the hunting fields. The word "noticeable" is not innocent. Indeed, these dogs, which were used mostly for hunting pheasants in Sologne, were very different from the descriptions written in books and specialized magazines. Most of the time, these Labradors, which were rapidly transformed into hounds, sought only to flush upland game or to fight with other dogs, while categorically refusing to submit to any kind of discipline. It was out of the question to ask them to fetch a wounded pheasant from thornbushes! The performance of these dogs was so disastrous that

Retrievers and blood searching

Some hunters have specialized their retrievers in tracking wounded game by following a trail of blood. It is true that these breeds have several advantages that predispose them to this work. Their nose is very powerful, they are used to trailing a wounded animal, and they are calm, steady, and able to concentrate. Furthermore, a retriever naturally puts its nose on the ground. However, this specialization quickly shows its limits. Thus, what will a

sweet Golden Retriever do in front of a wounded wild boar that has decided to exact a very high price for its tusks? Surely, retrievers are not aggressive enough to stand fast. On the other hand, certain bloodhounds are able to recapture a wounded deer, immobilize it, and sometimes even finish the kill. Here again, the Labrador is not able to do any of these tasks. It is better to reserve this work for breeds that are better suited for it.

many hunters took a dislike to them, asserting that their pointers were much better workers, which was undeniable. In fact, this deplorable situation is the result of a big misunderstanding. First, hunters made the mistake of being seduced by a dog they did not really know how to use. The Labrador is and always will be a specialist for retrieving, and is fit only for that. Wanting to make it quarter like a pointer is bound to produce disappointment. Indeed, it does this work like a very average spaniel. It quarters with its nose on the ground, whereas only by carrying its head high is it able to pick up

the scent of distant game. One must not be surprised to see it acting this way. First of all, the Labrador is a dog made to track a wounded bird. Moreover, by giving it the taste for hunting live game, its retrieving abilities are likely to fall off sharply. Indeed, it is very probable that the dog will prefer tracking upland game and flushing it to the more tedious work of fetching a dead bird. Thus, it will end up specializing in quartering live game and neglecting the rest. Finally, the Labrador will not quarter effectively because the way it covers the field is not at all methodical; he was never taught how to cut through the parcels of a

After the surge of popularity visited upon the Labrador, will the Golden Retriever undergo the same fate? The current infatuation with this superb dog leaves one fearful about this dog's future.

increasing demand of the marketplace. But they were rapidly overwhelmed by the less scrupulous. The result was not long in coming: today more than half of the Labradors are unfit for hunting.

All the same, the Labrador is still an excellent hunting dog, a specialist of retrieving in the purest British style. Nowadays, the Labrador Club seems to be returning to a more rigorously selective breeding by preferring working qualities, but the harm has been done. Would it be possible to imagine a better example of how a hunting breed can be destroyed by indiscriminate breeding? And it is not over

Above: A Labrador cut out for working has nothing to do with the veritable barrels on four legs seen strolling about on the sidewalks.

Opposite: A fearsome image of a predatory Labrador. His eyes alone should dispel the totally inapt image of "big teddy bear" that many human beings attribute to him.

territory without leaving anything to chance.

Hunters have made the mistake of buying Labradors without being concerned about their origins. In fact, from the start, many dog breeders completely neglected these animals' working qualities and concerned themselves only with the physical appearance of this dog. As a result, Labradors bred in such kennels could only be quite average hunters, at best. Did dog-show judges want heavier dogs with more square heads? No problem! Certain breeders went as far as secretly crossing Labradors and Rottweillers! It is easy to imagine how much damage these dogs produced on hunting fields. To be sure, a few breeders persistently followed their work of selective breeding based on serious criteria of working qualities, without taking into account the constantly

yet! Today, the Golden Retriever is drifting the same way as the Labrador. Tomorrow, it might be the Flat-Coated Retriever.

To choose the Labrador for a hunting dog is to acquire the services of a tremendous specialist for retrieving and fetching small wounded game, but the hunter who wishes to have a dog that can do everything would be better off leaning toward spaniels.

Continental Water Dogs: On the Road to Disappearance?

For a long time, European hunters used to have at their disposal water dogs specialized in hunting ducks and other waterfowl. These dogs, whose origins hark back to the Middle Ages, had the distinctive feature of having very dense and curly fur that was unusually effective in protecting them from the cold and from water. Both retrievers and spaniels at the same time, they flushed ducks and water hens from cover in reeds and retrieved shot game from rather deep water. Writings about hunting from the beginning of the nineteenth century bear witness to the effectiveness and the popularity of these helpers. They were so popular that Irish people developed a similar breed that brought together the same abilities: the Irish Water Spaniel.

But Continental water dogs were then rapidly forgotten and were supplanted by the success of more modern dogs: retrievers, spaniels, and pointers. This is unfortunate because they were tremendous dogs, courageous and with great endurance. For about a hundred years, they disappeared from hunting fields until a few people took the initiative to revive them. This is the case in France with the Barbet, a superb water dog of good size. But these attempts depend especially on "canine archeology": it is not sure that these dogs will renew their earlier success considering that hunters have formerly turned away from them.

Current attempts to save the hunting Barbet seem dubious, insofar as hunters are losing interest in this dog of the past.

Spaniels

Spaniels:
Dogs of Tomorrow?

Except for the English Cocker Spaniel, which is especially renowned for its qualities as a companion dog, spaniels are rather unappreciated in various European countries. However, on the British Isles, whence they originated, spaniels are the most numerous of British hunting dogs. If Continental hunters took so little interest in spaniels, it is surely due to the fact that they preferred using pointers, which are better suited for their hunting practices.

In Great Britain, hunters always needed dogs specialized in hunting small game in closed surroundings. Pointers, instead, were intended for fetching birds on extensive stretches of heathland, marshland, or cultivated fields. In addition

Continental spaniels?

All spaniels are of British origin and result from the specialization that is dear to the heart of the British people. However, in Germany there is a dog that could be classified as a spaniel: the Wachtelhund. This breed was established at the beginning of the century. Although its name means "quail dog," German hunters quickly specialized it in hunting all small game. Neither did they hesitate to use the Wachtelhund for hunting harmful animals and big animals. However, its style of active tracking and flushing makes it comparable to British spaniels.

to partridges, snipes, and grouses, the British Isles contain numerous small game, such as rabbits, woodcocks, and pheasants. But English hunters did not think it was worthy to hunt this game with pointers, because these animals moved in surroundings where the dog could not develop an ample and regular quartering. The favorite game of the English, pheasant was always hunted in great style, with a line of flushers that would

drive game toward a line of shooters. To do this, British hunters needed dogs that were very good in dense brush to run down game, rather than point it. Pheasants that are winged cannot run indefinitely. But the dogs also had to be excellent retrievers because this type of hunting produced a lot of wounded birds. To meet all these conditions, the British, who are extremely fond of dog breeding, developed spaniels, or rather, they adapted a type of dog to this very specific type of work.

The origin of these dogs is certainly the same as that of the Continental European spaniels: they are direct descendants from the longhaired setters of the Middle Ages. While French hunters, for example, were concerned with maintaining or even improving the dogs' abilities to point small game, Anglo-Saxons, who already had their own pointers, preferred yet another specialized breed. For this reason, they became interested in spaniels by developing different working qualities. These dogs had to demonstrate a swarming

Choosing a spaniel is less ostentatious than choosing a pointer, based more on practicality than on a concern with appearance.

The Cocker Spaniel, especially one with a golden coat, was so much in fashion in the 1970s with nonhunters that today many hunters fail to appreciate its talents as a good bush dog.

quartering perfectly adapted to brushy territory.

They also had to hunt very quickly, while always staying very close to their master to make game jump within close range of his gun. Thus, they had to rake the terrain methodically and penetrate the thickest thornbushes so that a rabbit or woodcock would have no chance left to escape.

As with pointers or retrievers, British hunters wanted to have very specialized dogs that would know perfectly how to accomplish a given task. However,

Following page: Surely, the Cocker Spaniel's success with hunters in the 1950s results from its effectiveness in tracking rabbits in thornbushes.

contrary to pointers and retrievers, spaniels are more versatile dogs. In this respect, they might be the most Continental of British dogs: they know how to find living game, how to make it leap or take flight, and how to retrieve it on the ground as well as in the water. But make no mistake: spaniels are not fit for those who hunt young partridges in plains or for those who are flushing pheasants. These hunters will have to use the services of two other types of dogs.

Today, spaniels are the dogs that hunters from the United Kingdom use the most. Perfectly adapted to the hunting practiced in England, spaniels still have good days ahead of them. Continental hunters who have had the opportunity to flush pheasants in the south of England or woodcocks in Ireland have certainly seen them perform and know that no other type of dog could do their work so effectively.

The Cocker Spaniel*

The Cocker Spaniel is such a nice dog that it was used as a model for the creation of the French comic strip, Boule and Bill, by a talented cartoonist. But one should not forget that the Cocker is above all, a hunting dog. If it is considered mostly as a companion, this is certainly because it was tremendously popular in the 1960s, as the Labrador is today.

Everybody wanted to have a Cocker at that time, especially the Golden kind, with a more or less dark beige color. The production of puppies that were not selectively bred rapidly burgeoned and the breed lost its hunting qualities quickly. Then, the Cocker almost exclusively took possession of sofas in living rooms and it developed a reputation that was not very enviable. It was reproached for its bad temper and growing aggressiveness with age. Let's be honest: this reputation was justified. Then other breeds started to attract the general public and they also suffered the plague of fashion, while the Cocker was

---

*The English Cocker Spaniel is known as the Cocker Spaniel in England. The dog known in the United States as the Cocker Spaniel is called the American Cocker Spaniel in other countries.

consigned to oblivion, at least in its role as companion dog. Some breeders, encouraged by the dynamic Cocker Spaniel Club, resumed the long and difficult work of selective breeding in order to bring the Cocker back onto the hunting fields.

It was an especially difficult task because in the meantime, the rabbit had almost disappeared, victim of myxomatosis. Before this terrible illness decimated the local rabbit population, many hunters were using the Cocker, which was considered as a fearless rabbit dog. But the disappearance of rabbits deprived the Cocker Spaniel of its main game. Accordingly, the restorers of the breed tried to make the Cocker a multipurpose dog to adjust it to the evolution of hunting. The bet paid off, in part.

The Cocker Spaniel is a very active dog in the field. It quarters in a swarming manner, giving the impression that it does not neglect an inch of land. Theoretically, it never strays far from its master and always hunts under the gun. Normally, the Cocker is a good retriever and does not hesitate to retrieve larger game, such as pheasants or hares. In fact, a Cocker in

the field sometimes evokes the sight of a hound.

Endowed with a strong character, the dog does not submit to blind authority easily, and training can be a little bit tricky. But once the training is successful, the dog is transformed into a wonderful helper that knows by turns how to flush pheasants, rabbits, and woodcocks. He does not hesitate to swim in order to go fetch a duck and even knows occasionally how to bark to alert the hunter when game is about to flee.

The Cocker is perfectly suited for group hunting of a variety of game in small territories. However, purchasing a puppy requires a scrupulous study of its origins because lineages that produce good hunting dogs are rare.

The English Springer Spaniel

Less well known than its cousin, the Cocker Spaniel, the Springer is better represented in the field. It is the most widely used hunting dog in Britain. It reigns supreme in battue hunting of grouses in highlands. It also dominates battue hunting of pheasants in England and accompanies almost all hunting guides (the gullies) in Ireland for woodcock and waterfowl hunting. In short, this is the supreme British hunting dog. Although its origins go back to the Middle Ages, its presence in many European countries is relatively recent. The first Springers appeared in, for example, France only after World War I.

In spite of his abilities, the Springer is not used very much in Continental Europe. It is an exceptional hunting dog that does not have the house-dog side that the Cocker Spaniel has. Few Springers are

The top hunting dog in Great Britain, the English Springer Spaniel is also the most versatile of British dogs.

owned by nonhunters. Because it is quite lively, this dog is not recommended for everyone. It hunts in a very sprightly way, literally bounding through the densest vegetation, hence its name.

Always close to its master, the Springer shows great courage in flushing pheasants, rabbits, or woodcocks from brambles. In these situations, pointers always show their limits and do not dare venture into vegetation that is too dense. When they show a little bit more boldness, they are rapidly stopped in their tracks when they catch scent of their prey and assume a beautiful pointing position. Unlike partridges in plains, small game will turn this pointing to an advantage. Assessing the situation perfectly, the

pheasant or rabbit will run off very quietly and escape harm, while the pointer loses time by creeping toward the game too fastidiously. The result is almost always the same: the game succeeds in slipping away without harm.

By contrast, the Springer throws game into a panic. The dog is everywhere at once, in front, behind, on the sides. The game, unable to identify the exact source of the danger, panics and rapidly flies away. The dog can also masterfully track the scent until literally upon the game, causing its prey to take flight and thereby giving its master his shot, because all the dog's work is done in close proximity to the hunter. The Springer's deadly effect-iveness makes some woodcock hunters

Either as flushers in large-scale battue hunts of pheasant, woodcock flushers in the bushes, snipe drivers in the bogs, or grouse flushers in the moors, English Springers know how to prove their effectiveness.

say that using a Springer might be too deadly and hence unfair in the hands of a less scrupulous hunter.

Like all spaniels, the Springer is well suited to contemporary conditions in which groups hunt small game. It is also well suited for the hunting currently practiced in the French Sologne region. In addition, this very precocious dog is easily trained, which is not to say that all training is superfluous. In France, the expansion of the breed was impeded by the quality of French breeding, which was mediocre for a long time. These dogs often had a strong, even uncontrollable, temperament. Fortunately, this problem is currently being resolved, especially among dogs born in French kennels where sires were generally bought from Irish or British hunting guides. Finally, the Springer has a definite advantage over other spaniels: most breeders produce true hunting dogs, not companion dogs.

In France, the Welsh Springer suffers from competition with the English Springer, which is better known among hunters. However, both of these dogs are fearless hunting dogs.

The Welsh Springer Spaniel

The English Springer has a close cousin: the Welsh Springer. For a long time, these two dogs were one, and it was only at the beginning of the twentieth century that the distinction between the two breeds was clearly established. Today, they are no longer at all the same dog. Their coats differ greatly: the Welsh Springer's is always white and red, whereas the English Springer's is brown and white or black and white. (Tan spots, however, are tolerated in both breeds.) The Welsh Springer is lighter than its cousin. These two dogs have neither the same hunting style nor the same temperament. As its name implies, the Welsh Springer was born from a region whose inhabitants are not renowned for their compliant character—on the contrary! True to its Welsh origins, the Welsh

Springer sometimes shows a certain stubbornness. It is more at ease in water than its English cousin. Without a doubt, it also has slightly better endurance, but is less inclined to fetch in bushes. Despite these minor differences, both dogs are equally effective, each in its own way. Unfortunately, there are few Welsh Springers, which limits the possibility of serious selective breeding based on working criteria.

The Clumber Spaniel

The use of this dog is not very widespread, neither in Contental Europe, Canada, the United States nor or in its native country. Supposedly it has French roots: in the eighteenth century, the Duke de Noailles is said to have offered a pair of this breed to the second Duke of Newcastle, who then resided in an estate called Clumber Park.

The Clumber, which can reach a weight of about 77 pounds (35 kilograms) for males, is the most imposing of the spaniels. Its powerful and bulky body conveys a sense of strength, not to say heaviness. Its coat is almost always white; only some lemon or orange spots on the head are accepted.

As a result of this morphology, the hunting rhythm of this spaniel is far from resembling that of the bounding Springer. It is rather a diligent and hard-working dog. One could compare it to a bulldozer that does not advance very quickly, but that nothing can stop. Most of the time, English hunters used it in packs during battue hunts of pheasant, to dislodge game gathered in impenetrable brush.

The Clumber Spaniel has a temperament that mirrors its physical appearance. It is calm but stubborn. If it resists its master's commands, it is rather out of inertia than impudence. Thus, training is a delicate task that requires a lot of patience. The Clumber must be given good reasons for performing a task and it is better to avoid subjecting it to overly strict discipline.

Today, even in England, it is very difficult to find a Clumber of quality because the number of these dogs is exceptionally low and the majority of these do not hunt. Thus, it is important to reflect long and hard before deciding to purchase this "museum piece."

The Clumber Spaniel is very rare in its native country and is almost nonexistent in Continental Europe, Canada, and the United States. This dog is no longer very well suited to contemporary hunting conditions, which are very far removed from the big pheasant shootings of the last century.

The Field Spaniel

Between the Springer and the Cocker is the Field Spaniel with an intermediate height. Although a powerful dog, it is not as heavy as the Clumber Spaniel. Its coat

The Field Spaniel (left) and the Sussex Spaniel (right) are two very rare breeds in Great Britain as on the Continent, as well as in the United States. The first one is a compromise between the Cocker and the Springer. The latter a supremely calm dog, is noted for the intensive use of its bark while hunting.

is almost always plain, with a liver, black, or roan color. Sometimes, it may be of two colors on a white background. Little tan spots are tolerated. With a proud and elegant gait, the Field Spaniel hunts diligently and methodically with its master. Its nose might be a little weak, compared to that of other spaniels. But like the Welsh Springer, the Field Spaniel shows great endurance.

The Field Spaniel has certainly suffered from the competition with the Cocker and the Springer, which has always kept the number of these dogs to a very low level. In France, for example, births never exceed a dozen puppies a year, a number surely insufficient to allow for rigorous selection of sires according to their working qualities. Thus, as with many other relatively rare dogs, this is an esoteric breed that needs to be approached with extreme caution. Its stronger population in its native country justifies importing them into Europe and North American judiciously.

The Sussex Spaniel

The Sussex Spaniel is a breed practically unknown among hunters. It looks a little bit like the Clumber, but is not as tall and has a lighter body. It has a calm temperament and was produced mostly to provide effective support to older hunters. Its coat is always a rich golden liver color with variation tolerated. The Sussex is a determined dog that hunts methodically. Its bark is its greatest characteristic. It uses its voice more than other spaniels, which made its reputation at the beginning of the century. The Sussex was believed to be able to modulate its barking according to the game that was flushed, which allowed the hunter to know in advance what game he was about to shoot.

To our knowledge, there are only a few dogs of this breed in Europe and in various countries, and records are no longer kept of the number of new births. In England, its native country, the breed

shows an alarming decline. There are strong odds that it will die out with the coming of the new millennium.

The Irish Water Spaniel

Here is an atypical spaniel. The Irish Water Spaniel is certainly the dog best suited for hunting waterfowl. Such is its reputation. Common to all breeds of water dogs from the last century, its curly and oily coat protects it from the harshness of the climate and freezing water. The peculiarity of its tail is that it is not covered by curly fur like the rest of the dog's body, but by short and wiry fur that makes the tail look like a rat's tail. Furthermore the Irish Water Spaniel uses its tail like a rudder in the same way as a nutria or a muskrat. This same type of fur covers the dog's cheeks and forehead. Its toes have a specially developed membrane that acts as a flipper. Its eyes are set far apart and at an oblique angle, which allows them to stay open under heavy rain or when the dog swims against a current. Of good height, it can move with great ease in marshes—no matter how thick or muddy.

The Irish Water Spaniel, a hunting dog with an active and dynamic temperament, is not simply a retriever, but also a dog that quarters in a very quick swarming manner, and which flushes teals and other waterfowl hidden in aquatic vegetation. It is a very well adapted water dog, but it is very difficult to maintain this breed in sufficient numbers.

In Continental Europe, there are only a dozen of these dogs. Breeders have many problems in finding sires that have real hunting qualities.

An atypical dog, the Irish Water Spaniel is the only example of a British breed copied from Continental breeds, using water dogs from the last century, like the Barbet, as models.

The Future of Spaniels

After having suffered—like the Irish Setter—from popularity, the Cocker Spaniel is gradually refining its ranks and is once again finding its way back to hunting fields.

If spaniels were originally hyper-specialized dogs, today they have an unquestionable future as all-around dogs. The evolution of hunting has certainly pushed many hunters to be interested in this type of breed.

Hunting at random, so dear to the hearts of many European men, is now a distant memory. Gone are the large fields well stocked with game where the hunter used to move around alone, shooting a partridge here, a rabbit there, as he liked.

For the most part, these vast common fields became completely deserted gloomy plains.

Hunters have also changed their habits. For professional reasons, they left the country to be closer to cities and now they encounter many difficulties when it comes to living with a city dog six days a week.

Hunting becomes a real problem and the first difficulty is to find a hunting territory close to a big city. Hunters hardly have any other choice but to turn to private or commercial hunting. Unfortunately, leases are so expensive that the cost of renting a few acres must be shared by several hunters. Then hunting is necessarily practiced in groups. Because game is rare and the hunters are so numerous, using birds raised in captivity is almost obligatory. Under these conditions, what is the use of Pointers?

Spaniels are perfectly well suited to these new practices. Being gun dogs, they avoid disturbing neighboring hunters in the line of beating game. It is useless to try to point pheasants that are going to run in the middle of thornbushes. It is better to run after them rigorously as spaniels do. Their retrieving must be perfect, because the number of game shot increases the chances of wounding game. Working in the water is also very important, because hunting these days almost invariably ends up near a body of water so the hunters can shoot a few mallards that the dogs will have to retrieve in the middle of the night. One might be tempted to say that spaniels are the perfect helpers to hunt birds that are not very wild. But one should distrust such impressions. Certainly, these hunting conditions allow a Springer or a Cocker to ten, the hunter could do the same work without using a dog (certainly with a little less pleasure). In fact, a dog justifies itself only as soon as its work becomes indispensable. The dog's task is to find and to put within range of its master's gun birds, rabbits, or hares that the hunter would not have had any chance to shoot without the dog. The current danger is the temptation

express itself honestly without conflicting with its true nature, which does not mean that it is made only for that. Like every hunting dog, spaniels show the true dimensions of their talents only when they face truly wild game, especially wild pheasant, which is born free in a territory where it must learn how to defend itself.

Indeed, game just released from captivity where they were bred hardly requires any searching. Nine times out of to classify spaniels as hunting dogs for pheasants raised in captivity, when they are altogether hunting dogs. They are able to hunt almost any game with as much effectiveness as pointers. They are not, on the one hand, the noble pointers of difficult game and, on the other hand, the flushers of pheasants bred in captivity. They are all hunting dogs but some of them adjust better than others to the unfortunate evolution in the practice of hunting.

Contrary to competitive events for pointers, field trials for spaniels remained closer to hunters'expectations and did not succumb to the attraction of pure competition.

Hounds

The Origin of Hounds

Previous pages: The Beagle-Harrier in the act of hunting a hare.

Compared to hounds, pointers and other retrievers are relatively recent types of hunting dogs. The origin of hounds goes back to prehistory, a period of time when men began to use dogs to help them hunt.

By carefully observing the hunting techniques of wolves and other wild dogs, men understood the usefulness of domesticating such mammals. The superior intelligence of these meat-eaters allowed men to tame them, but the fact that a wild species allowed itself to be put at the service of men remains a mystery in many respects. Only horses submitted to such domestication—and much more recently.

To explain the relationship between men and dogs, Native Americans thought that some kind of contract had been drawn up between man and beast. Dogs offered to guard men's property and to hunt at their side, in exchange for security and food so that the dog would not be entirely dependent on the hazards of hunting. Certain explorers also remark that dogs could be useful to men in a much more prosaic way—as food in case of famine!

The fact remains that the first hunting dogs were hounds. Since the time of the first writings, dogs were found at the side of humans, which leads one to assume that dogs were domesticated before this period. The appearance of the first narratives coincides with the end of

hunting as a method of subsistence, at least in Europe. Hunting became a sport and a symbol of power more than a necessity. From then on, hounds were the prerogative of nobles and lords. This was the beginning of hunting, whose history is embedded in the history of European sovereigns until the last century.

It is only recently that breeds, as we know them today, were defined. Before that, each region had its own type of dog, generally born from crossing different dogs brought back from journeys of war or trade. It might be interesting to relate the origins of each breed, but this would be more anecdotal than realistic, at least before the Middle Ages. At that time, all hounds were tall and robust with a coat that ranged from wiry hair, like the Shorthaired Griffon, to curly hair. The color of the coat did not matter very much.

Then certain lords, ardent hunting enthusiasts, selected types of dogs more specifically according to their taste and the particular abilities they were looking for in a dog. Thus the breeds were born. Among the first one could cite the *Chien blanc du roy* (the King's white dog) or the Saint Hubert, which were not very different from what they are today.

Although the selection of pointers was done very rigorously, breeds of hounds were not really fixed. Each huntsman continued to crossbreed his dogs without worrying about any official standard, his sole goal being to unite different abilities, which resulted in the largest stag-hunting packs looking rather unusual. Only with the emergence of dog breeding was a more precise selection process introduced, based on clearly defined morphological criteria.

breeds to themselves, forbidding their subjects from using such breeds. The end of monarchy led to a complete overthrow of such practices. Hounds that were previously considered a sign of power became the best symbol of popular hunting. Such a sudden change, unique in the history of dog breeding, corresponds to the advent of hunting with guns in

The evolution of how hounds were used is also surprising. As previously noted, these dogs were the privilege of lords for a long time, and some laws severely punished peasants who dared to own any. A few monarchs went so far as to reserve exclusive enjoyment of certain

southern European countries, particularly in France and Italy. Farmers who were the new owners of hunting rights selected smaller dogs from large breeds to hunt small and medium-sized furry game. A veritable explosion in the number of existing breeds followed. Each region,

Without a doubt it was by watching packs of wolves hunt that men got the idea of using packs of dogs for hunting.

Hunting with hounds is much more ancient than that of hunting with pointers. This miniature painting representing a Bloodhound is taken from The Hunting Book *by Gaston Phébus (1387).*

even each valley, had its own breed according to the local environment and the hunters' desires. But certain countries, like Great Britain, did not experience any such revolution, and hounds remained in the possession of noblemen to be used exclusively for stag hunting.

However, we should point out that most of these breeds were exported to the rest of Europe where they developed at an amazing rate. Once these breeds were introduced into France, for example, French farmers adopted them entirely and used them when hunting their favorite game with a gun: hares and wild boars. Even today, hound hunting of hares, rabbits, and even wild boars remains the most powerful symbol of a certain kind of popular hunting.

To summarize the history of hounds, one might say that they went from royal kennels to farmyards, while always remaining hunting dogs. Although this kind of hunting is no longer reserved for the nobility, it remains the prerogative of wealthy people for the most part, because maintaining a large pack of hunting dogs is not within the range of everyone's budget—far from it!

The Nevers Griffon, with the wolf-gray color of its coat, is surely the hound closest to the type of wolf dog used in the Middle Ages in France.

French Hounds:
An Incomparable Wealth

Without a doubt, France is the preeminent country of hounds. It is the cradle of hunting. The practice of hunting went beyond the level of simple entertainment for the nobility and reached the level of a veritable art. To be convinced of this, one need only consider the impressive number of books on hunting techniques and dogs that have been published for many centuries.

There is an incredible variety of breeds of hounds in France: more than twenty-five breeds are recorded, whereas fewer than a dozen breeds, at the most, exist in other countries. Despite their number, each French breed has a specific use. They were created to be suitable for hunting methods practiced on very specific types of game and terrain. In France, hunting with hounds is done in many ways. Certainly, firearm hunting with hounds is the most common hunting style today: one or several dogs are set on the track of furry animals that can then be shot when they flee.

This basic principle is obviously suitable for hard-to-find game. Hare hunting, which is done almost exclusively south of the Loire River on relatively wide fields, calls for fast dogs with a fine nose. Wild-boar hunting with hounds is practiced mainly in hilly areas with sparse vegetation and in semimountainous areas. More recently, hounds have been used to hunt deer, but hunting rabbit with hounds remains their most frequent use and it is this form of hunting that enthuses the greatest number of hunters.

Far from being abandoned, hunting with the aid of hounds continues to attract many sportsmen. Packs that hunt deer are concentrated north of the Loire River, close to the big forests. The tradition of large-game hunting on horseback with hounds is maintained with more difficulty south of the Loire. Huntsmen are less interested in hunting deer, which is difficult to hunt on horseback using a pack of hounds.

France has always been the country with the most abundant number hounds (here, a Small Blue Gascony).

Hunters often return with an empty bag (saying then that the bush was empty). Packs of hounds called boar-hounds are also used to hunt wild boars.

In addition to hunting large game on horseback with hounds, hounds are also used for small game hunting *(la petite vénerie),* most commonly hares. While packs of hounds for large-game hunting are

Opposite: This fawn Basset of Brittany well illustrates the passion that hunters have for rabbit hunting with small hounds.

Following page: The history of hounds in France began with horseback hunting using a pack of hounds [la grande vénerie], which developed in France to an extent unattained in any other country.

losing ground because of the difficulty of maintaining numerous dogs and horses, hunting smaller game with hounds is thriving. This type of hunting is done most typically on foot with a limited pack. This is a difficult and athletic form of hunting—difficult because the hare is very sly and shows considerable ingenuity in leaving its pursuers behind. Moreover, hares are fast and their scent is light. It is an athletic form of hunting because hunters must try to follow their dogs to back them up at critical moments, which means that the hunter must run indefinitely over long distances.

Rabbit hunting is also becoming more popular in some countries because it requires fewer dogs and less territory. However, rabbits are not easy to hunt, and to succeed, both dogs and huntsmen have

to show a lot of insight. Fox hunting, which is not practiced very much elsewhere, remains the specialty of British huntsmen.

The variety of breeds of hounds, then, is due not only to these different methods of hunting, but also to the very diversified types of terrain in France. From the orderly forests of central France to the sandy moors of the west, passing along the

sun-drenched hills and other semiarid areas of the south, dogs are out through different tests. In one region they have to be resistant to frost, in another, to rain, and in another, to heat. The relief of the terrain might be more or less mountainous. One can better understand why hounds from Brittany are not the same as those from the south of France.

Today, unlike the case with pointers, the great variety of French hounds is not a handicap. Surely, certain breeds tend to disappear, but others that were developed recently are very successful, such as the Anglo-French breed used in hunting small game.

The position of France in terms of hounds is unique in the world.

Hounds Used for Rabbit Hunting:
A French Tradition

There are two sizes of Griffon Bassets from the Vendée region: the Large Basset and the Small Basset. The first is more specifically suited for rabbit, hunting whereas the second can hunt hares equally well.

Is there a species of game more popular or more typically French than rabbits? Of course not, and rabbiting remains the form of hunting most frequently practiced in France. Rolled during a flush for game, tumbled under the nose of a pointer, or shot while breaking cover, rabbits are the objects of countless hunts. The most interesting way to hunt rabbits by far is to use hounds. In a small covered field, dogs patiently go back and forth as they follow the scent of a rabbit that plays games with

its pursuers and loses them in endless detours. Hunters take up position at spots where they assume the rabbit will pass and follow the careful work of their dogs.

The French seem to be the only ones to have produced breeds of dogs specifically suited for this type of game. These are generally hounds from which the smallest subjects were selected. In the end, new breeds were created that have all the characteristics of Bassets.

The Artesian Basset of Normandy

The Artesian Basset of Normandy could be defined as a calm and steady but stubborn and resistant dog. This beautiful short-haired dog with long ears and a sweet look has been popular for a long time. City dwellers became very fond of the breed and it gained its place among the companion dogs.

Fortunately, the Artesian Basset of Normandy Club knew how to preserve the dog's working abilities. Today, it is the most widespread French hound. Not very fast, it never loses its cool and patiently unravels the convoluted tracks made by an especially capricious rabbit. This nice-looking dog is far from being apathetic and is always willing. Under this serene appearance is a devouring passion for

hunting; tireless, it has more endurance than speed. Because of its very good temperament, this is one of the rare hounds that can live in a city.

The Fawn Brittany Basset

From its famous ancestor, the Fawn Griffon, the Fawn Brittany Basset inherited an ardor that nothing can stop. This breed's intrepid character reveals remarkable power and speed. It has retained a specific characteristic from its native region. This animal's small height (it is the smallest hound) has made it a specialist in rabbit hunting. Its coarse coat serves as protection from the thickest thorns and especially from the sandy moors of Brittany. All these qualities make it a modern dog that many hunters would like to have. Hunters from the south of France, who have just recently discovered this little dog are very happy with it because it has adjusted perfectly to the scrubby terrain of the region. For this reason, Fawn Brittany Bassets are very numerous south of the Loire River. Several successful results in

The Artesian Basset of Normandy is the only French hound that has met with significant success with the general public, mainly because of its elegance.

advanced field trials and an intelligent policy by the Fawn Brittany Basset Club promise a great future for these dogs.

The Petit Basset Griffon Vendéen

The history of the Petit Basset Griffon Vendéen (or Little Griffon Basset of the Vendée) is closely linked to that of the Dezamy family, which, during the first half of the twentieth century, became passionate about breeding this dog and made it a breed independent from the other griffons of the Vendée region.

Since its appearance, the Petit Basset is dedicated exclusively to rabbit hunting, an exercise in which it excels. Its small height and hard coat allow it to creep

Above: The Fawn Brittany Basset is the favorite rabbit hound of French hunters, who willingly forgive its extreme character and appreciate its passionate temperament.

Opposite: The Little Griffon Basset of the Vendée region is the direct rival of the Fawn Brittany Basset in the hearts of French rabbit hunters. Its hunting style, close to that of hounds, is, however, quite different.

through the worst kind of thorns that would discourage shorthaired dogs. Its voice is superior to that of many other bassets and the tricks it uses in trapping game are always interesting. This basset's character is a little difficult, and requires patience and skill, but its master must channel the dog's character and not stifle it. Along with the Beagle and the Fawn Brittany Basset, the Little Griffon Basset is the most widespread hound in France.

The Blue Gascony Basset

The Blue Gascony Basset was developed at the beginning of the century to hunt rabbits. Its way of tracking this game makes it look like an extremely methodical dog. Hugging the track, it shows a good

nose and announces its progress with impressive howling barks. This is certainly the main interest of this dog.

This breed was never really successful and there have never been very many of these dogs. At the end of World War II, the Blue Gascony Basset was almost on its way to extinction. But in the 1970s, a few breeders, supported by the breeding club, led a comeback and increased the height and the vivacity of this dog. Its short hair and fine nose make it capable of hunting on dry and rocky terrains. Thus, the Gascony is perfectly at ease in the fields of the south of France, where unfortunately rabbits, its favorite prey, are becoming rare.

Despite commendable efforts by enthusiasts and a dynamic club, the Blue Gascony Basset cannot manage to attract hunters. The number of these dogs remains low.

French Beagles

There is a category of hounds that are quite taller than the bassets: the French beagles. These dogs, which include many different breeds, were largely used for firearm hunting. Another reason that explains hunters' infatuation with French beagles is their tremendous versatility.

Originally created for hunting hares or hunting with a pack, beagles showed themselves as being perfect for hunting deer and wild boar. The increase in these two kinds of game led to renewed interest in these dogs, at a time when hares became rare in the French countryside. There is no doubt that French beagles are the future hounds for big-game hunting.

This category of dogs includes different "families." The most important is certainly that of the French beagles from the south of France. Born from a cross between dogs of rank and beagles from the country, these dogs are perfectly adapted to the dry and hot lands and thickets of the south of France. The next category of beagle, developed in the west of France, is more rough and thick-coated and therefore able to maneuver perfectly in the bushy terrain of sandy moors without losing its elegance.

Finally, there are dogs born from hunting on horseback using a pack of hounds, which are specialized in tracking hares.

The Ariège Beagle

The Ariège is the archetype of the French beagle. It is the result of a cross between big dogs of rank, like the Saintonge Gascony or the Blue Gascony, and unpedigreed beagles from the country, which were ferocious hare hunters. This mixture produced results that met breeders' expectations.

Both docile and calm like a big stag-hunting dog, the Ariège is patient and not very fast, but is as crafty as a mutt. Perfectly at ease in the rocky and dry lands in southern France, it was able to win over many hunters for its wild-boar hunting and remains a perfect helper for hunting hare in moderately mountainous terrains.

The Small Blue Gascony

The Small Blue Gascony remains very close to its counterpart, the Large Blue Gascony. What prompted its development was the desire of hunters to have a smaller pack dog. A specialist of hare hunting in southwest France, this dog, which is characterized by its superb voice, almost disappeared until it was discovered again with the growth in wild-boar hunting. Today, although there are not very many of these dogs, they are increasing in numbers. Its resistance to heat has enabled it to attract hunters from southern Europe.

On the hunting field, the Small Blue shows the same qualities as dogs of rank, that is great docility and endurance.

The Small Blue Gascony is a truly reduced model of dogs used in packs by hunters on horseback. Needless to say, it is diligent, works well in a pack, and is disciplined.

Previous page: The Ariège Beagle is a hare hunter specialized in hunting in the mountains, with all the attendant difficulties of terrain and climate.

The Blue Gascony Griffon cannot seem to attract hunters, who often prefer griffons from the Vendée region or from Brittany, although its ability to work in dense undergrowth is the same.

The Blue Gascony Griffon

Not very well known by hunters, the Blue Gascony Griffon has certainly suffered from competition with other griffons, which has prevented it from attaining national recognition. It is the only beagle from southwestern with a griffon-type coat making this dog particularly apt for wild-boar hunting in the most impenetrable sun-drenched hills. But in cases of extreme heat its thick coat is a sure handicap.

Recently, the Blue Griffon won some success in field trials, which brought it back to prominence, but, it looks as though these achievements will be short-lived.

However, this dog has more than one quality; in particular its versatile voice, which is sometimes a howl and sometimes a deeper rumble. It also has immense stamina and an excellent nose.

The Little Saintonge Gascony

The Saintonge Gascony is the only dog that was created from crossing two purebreeds without any further blood mixing. In the middle of the last century, the Baron of Carayon de la Tour developed this new breed by crossing the last dogs of Saintonge with Large Gascony Blues. He obtained a dog that possesses the qualities of both breeds. Thus, like the Large Gascony Blue, the Little Gascony is

fast and impetuous, but it is also diligent and shrewd, as the dogs of Saintonge were.

This breed includes two varieties of dogs characterized by their height, but this distinction was not made until much later because these two dogs are almost identical. Today, the bigger one is dying out: it is no longer used in packs by hunters on horseback. The few dogs that still exist are used to reinvigorate other breeds. On the other hand, the small one is having renewed success, because of large-game hunting with the aid of hounds. But it is not used very much by hare huntsmen, who find it a bit slow.

The Fawn Brittany Griffon

In addition to the beagles from the south of France, which all have more or less the same qualities, in the west of France, there are hounds with the same body that present their own characteristics. Thus, the Fawn Brittany Griffon is the heir of the Great Fawn of Brittany, which is extinct today, but which was formerly used in packs to hunt wolves in the sandy moors of Brittany in the last century. From this ancestor, the Fawn Griffon kept a taste for difficult game. It has a keen nose and is vigorous and tireless, no matter what working terrain is imposed on it. Today, this dog is especially used for battue hunting of deer

Above: The Fawn Brittany Griffon is the descendant of Great Griffons that used to hunt wolves in the sandy gorse moors in Brittany in the last century before this extraordinary animal became extinct.

Left: The Saintonge Gascony is the famous heir of a prestigious breed that has disappeared: the Saintonge. Like its ancestor, the Saintonge Gascony is in a precarious situation because so few of them exist.

and wild boar. Courageously steadfast it shrinks from nothing and shows great temerity before the "black beast" (wild boar). A little difficult in character, it demands firm authority from its master. It is also renowned for its fox hunting, which is currently very popular in its native region.

The Griffon from the Vendée Region (Large Basset and Beagle)

The Great Basset Griffon from the Vendée region was born out of the desire of hunters to develop a relatively tall basset that was capable of specializing in tracking hares. As for the Griffon Beagle, it is the result of a selective breeding to reduce the height of the Great Griffons from the Vendée region in order to obtain a dog fit for hunting hares in packs.

Thus, these two griffons from the Vendée region were created to hunt the same game. Without a doubt, the Great Basset is more docile than the Beagle, which some people consider very difficult to discipline. With their griffon coat, these two dogs have no difficulty dealing with the sandy moors of their native country. Both won fame in large-game hunting as well in fox hunting.

The Porcelain

Under this fragile-sounding name is hidden a rustic and resistant dog. The Porcelain, which is distinguished by its great speed, looks like a French hound of medium size.

Originally created in the Franche-Comté region for hare hunting, this superb dog almost disappeared during the twentieth century. But in the 1970s, a handful of enthusiasts increased the

The Beagle Griffon from the Vendée region is taller than the Basset Griffon from the Vendèe region. Like the Fawn Brittany Griffon, packs of these dogs used to hunt wolves in the thickets of the Vendée region in the last century.

numbers of dogs belonging to this breed. Its keen nose and speed, which were improved thanks to infusions of British blood, attracted a large number of hunters.

Today, the Porcelain hunts wild boars and especially deer, but its great specialty remains hare hunting, in which it really excels.

The Artois Dog

Watch out! This breed is on the road to extinction. This dog carries on its robust shoulders the prestigious past of the great Artois Dogs, which won fame toward the end of the Middle Ages as pack hounds kept by aristocratic hunters in northern France.

Specialized in tracking hares, the Artois Dog had its hour of glory during the last century. However, multiple cross-breedings that were supposed to improve it brought about its downfall. The dog lost its inherent qualities and consequently fell out of favor with hunters.

Today, certain breeders are trying to revive this breed, but without much success. This is regrettable because this rustic dog, with endurance and above all a very keen nose, could have satisfied many hunters.

The Nevers Griffon

It is sometimes difficult to imagine what hounds from the Middle Ages were like, because successive reintroductions, cross-breedings, and fusions of breeds greatly altered the dogs' appearance over the centuries. But the Nevers Griffon, a big rustic dog with hair typical of griffons and a "wolf-gray" colored coat, always remained true to its origins.

Bottom left: Despite its name and slightly affected attitude, the Porcelain is not a fragile dog. It is undoubtedly one of the most extraordinary hare-hunting dogs because of its speed and keen nose.

Below: Today the Artois Dog is in decline. In the last century, however, it was one of the favorite breeds of French huntsmen who praised its calm, endurance, and reliable nose.

Griffon is hardly used anymore in big packs, it is appreciated more and more by battue hunters of wild boar and deer.

The Anglo-French Hound of Small-Game Hunting

Although most French hound breeds are very ancient, the Anglo-French Hound is very recent. This dog is the result of planned breeding by hare huntsmen and also wolf hunters who sought to produce dogs that were easy to train like pedigrees and who had the modern qualities of British dogs. In fact, the breed had already existed for a long time when the Anglo-French Club was founded about fifteen years ago.

Today, because of dog fanciers and especially hunters, the A.F.P.V. (l'Anglo Français de Petite Vénerie) [The Anglo-French of Small Game Hunting], as they like to call it, is the most appreciated dog of its category. No doubt its success will increase in the years to come.

The Beagle-Harrier

Contrary to what the name implies, the Beagle-Harrier is not a British dog but entirely French. Originating at the beginning of the century, this dog came from crossing the Beagle and the Harrier, but it also comes from beagles of southwestern France. Hare huntsmen who used beagles found that they were not always tall enough and thus encountered serious difficulties in many overcoming the obstacles in sandy moors and in crossing drainage canals. Although many disapproved of the union of the Beagle and the Harrier, it allowed the improvement of the Beagle's speed and

Above: The Nevers Griffon has had mixed luck.

Above: The Anglo-French of small-scale hunting is a very recent breed that symbolizes the renewal of hounds.

Today, it hunts wild boars as it used to hunt wolves or deer in the past, with the same courage and endurance. This very ancient breed has exceptionally homogenous qualities, and one can find the characteristics peculiar to the Nevers Griffon in every dog of this breed. Although the Nevers

endurance. Unfortunately, this dog was subject to differences of opinion among breeders, who constantly wanted to make it more like either one or the other of its progenitors. For the past fifteen years, the French Beagle-Harrier Club has taken the matter in hand and has imposed a breeding policy that tends to stabilize the breed, which now specializes in tracking deer. Its coat is fairly short and flat, and often tricolored.

Although the Beagle-Harrier was developed for hare hunting in southwestern France, today it has proved to be an excellent wild boar hunter, which might give it the boost that it has always lacked.

Dogs Used in Packs
for Hunting on Horseback

In France, hunting on horseback using a pack of hounds has created a number of breeds unmatched in the world. Paradoxically, French hunters did not want to keep local breeds for big hunts, and most of the local dogs tend to become rarer, to the benefit of a few national breeds. Hounds that were bred for use in the great packs tended to be crossed with British breeds more liberally than with other hounds.

The number of dogs intended for the big hunts is relatively low, because today not many packs of hounds hunt large animals. Nevertheless, hunters converted a certain number of these dogs into suitable dogs for hunting deer, wild boar,

and stags. It should be noted that breeders of these dogs are nonexistent because each pack of hounds produces the dogs it needs.

The Great Griffon from the Vendée Region

Nowadays there are no more packs of hounds that use the Griffon from the Vendée region for hunting big game. Hunters were most likely attracted by the qualities of more recent breeds and had certainly gotten tired of its difficult character. Impetuous and fiery, the Great Griffon always had difficulty submitting to the rigorous discipline that a large hunting pack demands. With more endurance than speed, this dog, nevertheless, performed wonders when hunting wolves or wild boars in the sandy moors of the northern Atlantic coast.

Presently, very few of these dogs remain, although certain hunters still use it for shooting wild boar and deer. One must admit that hunters prefer the Beagle over the Great Griffon from the Vendée region.

The Billy

This tall dog of rank is not originally from Great Britain. Its name comes from the property of its creator M. G. Hublot du Rivault, a hunter from the Poitou region who was very fond of hunting hares. Very quickly, huntsmen used it for horseback hunting using pack hounds and made it a specialist in tracking hares. They worked hard at increasing its size so that it would

The Billy is the last descendant of the king's white dogs.

*Above, left: The Poitevin (from
the Poitou region), a "noble
mongrel," is a very distinguished
dog whose origins are more
than uncertain. It successfully
went from hunting wolves, to
hunting stags.*

*Right: The Great Blue Gascony
is a traditional hunting dog in
southwestern France that is no
longer used in big packs.*

*Previous pages: In hunting with
packs, the hunter and his
horse are of small importance
compared to the dog pack,
which is the very reason for
the existence of this type
of hunting.*

become as tall as the other dogs of good
pedigree. Indeed, the Billy is not as
famous as certain pack hounds used for
hunting on horseback, but this typical
French breed has a certain something that
attract masters of pack hounds who are
looking for fast dogs to hunt small deer.

The Poitevin

Hunting wolves with packs of dogs made
its fame in the Haut-Poitou region. It is
also in this region that the most beautiful
pedigree designed to hunt this big prey
was born. Not too heavy, the Poitevin
remained a dog with great elegance. With
both a keen nose for tracking deer and
great speed in tracking stags, it became
specialized in hunting these two types of
game. It has withstood the competition of

other pedigreed dogs and maintained its
numbers in many packs.

The Great Blue Gascony

The last big packs of hounds that
unleashed the Great Blue Gascony disappeared a long time ago and with them,
the tradition of tall pedigreed dogs from
the southwest died out as well. Today,
only a few hare hunters, nostalgic for a
splendorous past, still use them.

This breed has a prestigious past.
Henry IV, among others, swore by the
Great Blue for hunting wolves. In the
course of time, speed became more and
more important for huntsmen and the
Great Blue is now considered too slow
and heavy as a pack hound for large-game
hunts. This is regrettable, because this

beautiful French breed was part of French heritage. Today, it is difficult to imagine this dog ever making a comeback.

The Great French

There are three different breeds of Great French, which are distinguishable by the color of their coat: white and black, tri-colored, and white and orange.

These three dogs appeared quite recently, the first two dating from 1957, and the third from 1978. All three were produced by the selective breeding of Anglo-French dogs. Huntsmen wanted to bring the French type out by using dogs from the south of France for the white-and-black dog, the Poitevin and the Billy for the tricolored dog, and the Billy for the white-and-orange dog.

These dogs have been specialized in tracking deer, where they show great effectiveness. They have a typically French style of hunting that favors meticulous work over speed.

The Great Anglo-French

The Great Anglo-French is a breed that does not really exist. Indeed, huntsmen have always crossed breeds between themselves to reconcile the qualities of each without taking standards into account. Also, as its name points out, the Anglo-French is the result of mixing British and French dogs. Thus, there is not one Anglo-French but several, according to the dogs that were used.

Today, the majority of large packs of hounds are composed of Anglo-French.

Above left: By repeatedly crossbreeding French dogs with British dogs, huntsmen ended up forgetting the characteristics inherent in their national breed. Hoping to restore these traits, certain huntsmen worked on selecting French breeds. The Great French are the result of this research.

Right: In France, the Great Anglo-French are the most widely used dogs for large-game hunting packs.

British Hounds:
Always Faster!

The Harrier was born from the desire to have a tall dog for hunting foxes with pack hounds. This dog would have the same qualities as a hunter as the Beagle does.

As for pointers, the British hunter's idea of the usefulness of hounds is quite different from that of Continental European hunters. Hunting takes on a very special form in England. Nowadays, only two game are hunted: hares and foxes. When hare hunting is practiced, which is becoming less and less frequent, it is done with one of the most popular breed of hounds—the Beagle. On the other hand, fox hunting is still very much practiced. It is important to understand that British hunting is far from being like hunting elsewhere. More than pure hunting, it is principally a horse-riding

exercise. The difficulties that the riders might encounter during these frantic rides represent the first center of interest for the British. For many of them, the pleasure of hunting is secondary.

Thus, breeds of hounds were especially created for galloping as fast as possible. These dogs, which often hunt by sight, are far from being excellent trackers. Their barking is often weaker than breeds from other countries. On the other hand, they are fast, have great endurance, and gather themselves very well. European, and later the North American huntsmen did not fail to notice their qualities. They always owned a few British dogs in their kennels, for reinvigorating their own packs. It is nevertheless worth noting that shooting game with the help of hounds does not exist in Great Britain.

The Beagle

The end of the Middle Ages marks the beginning of the Beagle's history in its native country. Very quickly, the breed had success with British hunters who hunt hares, which was called beagling.

In the middle of the last century, the Beagle was brought to other European countries as a specialist in tracking hares. However, hunters quickly took possession of this dog to make it a fearless rabbit hunter. More recently, the development of

The Beagle, one of the most widespread hounds in Europe, is used for rabbiting as well as flushing big game.

big game in Europe, especially France and Germany, again offered a supplementary field of action for this wonderful short hound. With an adequate bark and a sufficient nose, the Beagle is an outgoing dog. A docile animal, he accepts discipline easily. Its great versatility and the fact it does not take up much space certainly explain why it is an extremely popular hound today in Europe, Canada, and North America. Its numbers continue to increase.

The Basset Hound

The Basset Hound, the only British hunting basset, is especially known today as a companion dog. Originally develped for hare hunting, this dog has French roots. Moreover, its hunting style is rather close to

the style of French bassets. When it sticks to tracking, it bays beautifully, and compensates for its average speed with a great endurance, which is belied by its appearance. In Europe, the Basset Hound is used mostly for rabbit hunting. Its moderate proclivity for working in thornbushes might lead it more toward flush hunting of deer, for which it shows great effectiveness.

The Harrier

This very old British breed has always met with only modest success. Although in its native country the Harrier is one of the two incontestable specialists of fox hunting by packs, its use in Europe was for a long time confined to the hunting of hares. Later on, it was used for roe buck and even wild-boar shooting, where it showed surprising courage.

Very fast, it was perfectly fit for fox hunting, because its speed allows it not to lose the fleeting trail of the fox. Very docile and gathering well in the pack, the Harrier is an easy-to-manage dog, which compensates for its lack of a strong voice. The Harrier suffers from the competition of other breeds, and unfortunately, it has not met with the success in various European countries and North America that it deserves. Furthermore, today it suffers from the fierce competition of the Anglo-French of Small Game Hunting.

The Foxhound

If there is a dog perfectly adapted to the difficult exercise of fox hunting, it is indeed the Foxhound. Hunting at a phenomenal speed, it is able to maintain a constant pace for long hours, and rare are the riders who are able to follow its pace until the end. It has a weak nose and voice, but compensates for these handicaps by always keeping the animal in sight, which does not have time to leave its pursuers behind. The build of the Foxhound is a little reminiscent of the pointer's, but the Foxhound has more bulk. Its head can also be compared to that of the prestigious pointer. There are no particular colors for this dog, because its skeletal structure is all that counts. It is not very common.

Above: The Basset Hound is the most French of the British hounds. Its origins can be found on the Continental side of the Channel. Do not be mistaken by its nonchalant appearance; it is a passionate hunter.

Other Hounds

The tradition of hunting was maintained in particular in France and in Great Britain. But it is not very common in other European countries, and as a result, fewer hounds are registered in those other countries.

However, there are still some prestigious breeds that are the fruits of a distant hunting past or of the more recent hunting past when hunters began using firearms. In many countries, only one or two breeds can be found. All the same, some of these breeds have succeeded in achieving international fame.

The Saint Hubert (Hound)

The Saint Hubert is surely the most impressive of the hounds. Its big size, drooping features and black-and-tan coat are the main reasons for this spectacular appearance. The most remarkable aspect of this dog is its exceptional voice, which cannot leave anyone indifferent.

It has very ancient origins. Monks from the abbey of Saint Hubert in the Belgian part of the Ardennes mountains supposedly raised it in memory of their saint. At the end of the Middle Ages, it was the favorite dog of kings and noblemen who hunted stags. It was gradually abandoned because it was considered too slow and too tall.

At the same time, breeders sprang up in both Great Britain and the United States, where it is called the Bloodhound. He was made into a companion dog but also into a dog specialized in searching for people.

To save the breed from extinction, it was necessary to import some of them again to Europe. With an exceptional nose and great calm, this dog is no longer used for hunting, although it could render great services as a blood tracker or as a retriever of wild boar.

The Bruno Jura Hound

There are two varieties of the Bruno Jura Hound. The Bruno type is a relatively tall dog for a Beagle. Its black-and-tan coat is reminiscent of the Saint Hubert's, as well as its build with drooping features. It is decidedly less widespread, however.

The Bruno Jura Hound was developed to hunt various game in the Alps. With a great sense for hunting and a staunch endurance and resistance, it has a strong voice and gathers easily in the pack. It is also a very versatile dog that allows the hunter to have only one or two small packs. Nothing more was needed to make it successful among hare hunters in, especially, France, but also, more recently among hunters of wild boars and roe bucks.

The Saint Hubert is perhaps the best-known hound in Europe, especially in France, Belgium, and the Netherlands. It is also without a doubt the most impressive. Unfortunately, with certain exceptions, it is hardly used anymore for hunting. In the United States this impressive breed is often called Bloodhound.

One should know that there are other varieties of Swiss Hounds that are part of the same breed but which are not very common.

Bloodhounds

Although usually classified among hounds, Bloodhounds are, however, quite distinct from them. This category is comprised of two breeds: the Hanover and the Bavarian.

The Hanover Bloodhound is the tallest and the oldest. Its origins go back to the seventeenth century. From the start, it was used in searching for large wounded game. The Bavarian Bloodhound is both smaller and more recent. Today, it is the most common Bloodhound because it has proved that it can hunt any kind of game, but even so there are not many of these dogs.

The German club devoted to both breeds was concerned about preserving the true qualities of this dog and for this reason issues a limited number of authorizations for owning a Bavarian or a Hanover. People who prove that they know blood tracking well and that they have the possibility of going out in the fields often can obtain these authorizations.

The French Bavarian and Hanover Bloodhounds Club has a policy of selecting sires and overseeing births. This policy is the guarantee of a future—surely slightly confidential—but serious and a guarantee of the effectiveness of these two breeds. The amateur who wishes to bypass this exiguous trial to obtain a puppy of this breed may instead purchase it at one of the few breeders who do not belong to the club. This means taking a big risk concerning the future use of the dog and it also encourages a dishonest practice, to say the least.

There are several Swiss Hounds that represent different varieties of the same breed. The Bernese is one of them, like the Bruno Jura Hound.

Above: The Bavarian Bloodhound is an impressive dog that does not invite petting. However, its calm is legendary. Its exceptional abilities make it an expert specialist in searching for large wounded game.

Opposite: The Bruno Jura Hound, originally from Switzerland, is mainly used today by French hunters. It should be said that Swiss laws, very restrictive in terms of hunting, do not allow the use of hounds anymore in favorable conditions.

Dachshunds

Dachshunds:
A Breed Apart

Previous pages: Tracking is one of the multiple specialties of the Dachshund. This dog is restless in the search for a large wounded animal. The hunter will unleash the dog close to the animal. The chase begins and will end with the dog in a steady position.

In a backpack, the Dachshund knows how not to call attention to itself. It will get out at the end of a flush hunt of big game to check each spot at which the hunter fired upon his prey. This enables the hunter to know whether there is a wounded animal in the field.

The Dachshund is in a category unto itself among hunting dogs. He is neither a hound [although the AKC and the KC (GB) group this breed under the Hounds] nor a terrier, nor a retriever, even less a spaniel; in brief the Dachshund is unique.

Originally German, the breed of Dachshund, which means "badger dog," goes back to the Middle Ages. The first tracks of this dog can be found back in the sixteenth century in a book by Jacques du Fouilloux entitled *La Vénerie* [Venery]. But the small dogs of the Basset type are much more ancient and go back to antiquity. Century after century, hunters from beyond the Rhine River conceived the Dachshund as a perfectly versatile dog. Its standard, which was written in 1879, was the first one to be elaborated in history.

The Dachshund hunts hares and rabbits by leading hunters to its prey with its bark. It is also a wonderful helper for searching big wounded game. But it can also flush big game with its bark, with very good results. It can also flush pheasants and retrieve them after the shooting. However, its favorite domain remains hunting underground. Although in theory it can do anything, it could be a mistake to believe that it is able to replace a Cocker Spaniel, a Labrador, a Bavarian Bloodhound, or a Griffon from the Vendéen region. At the most, it might

render a few services beyond blood tracking, digging up game, and flush hunting. Nevertheless, today it is the ideal dog for a hunter who practices only big game shooting or big game stalking. Someone who has never seen a Dachshund in action during a flush hunt has considerable difficulty imagining such a small dog staying staunch in front of a beast that weighs a couple of hundred pounds and that can be rendered particularly aggressive by its wound. However, it is an extraordinary sight to see this small dog harassing the monster with its piercing barking, while staying always at a respectable distance and expertly avoiding the animal's charges.

In fact, given its short size, the Dachshund shows exceptional courage. But its great temerity is always tinged with prudence, especially when it hunts underground, where in complete darkness, it has to confront the claws of a badger or the mouth of a female fox alone.

Although certain dogs are able to attack an animal head-on, the hunters who hunt such game that takes refuge in burrows tend to look for careful dogs that are content to lead the hunter to his prey with their bark alone, without systematically looking for a confrontation: this is because one day the wild animal will inevitably be the strongest. Nonhunters are often surprised by the snarling side of the

Dachshund, but they fail to realize that this aggressive behavior comes from a long selection built mainly upon the courage of these dogs, which, as previously mentioned, are confronted with dangerous hunting situations.

In France, the Dachshund was first used as an underground hunting dog. In the 1950s, a few French soldiers who were posted in Germany discovered this dog among the local hunters, and they brought it back to France. Dachshunds showed their effectiveness rapidly.

There are three varieties of Dachshunds:

• The wirehaired Dachshund is the most frequently used for hunting. Its thick coat protects it against the thickest bushes.

• The short- or smooth-haired Dachshund had its hour of glory above all as a companion dog in the 1970s.

• The longhaired Dachshund, the most elegant, seems more feminine than masculine. However, the three of them are able to hunt with the same effectiveness.

Moreover, there are three different miniature Dachshunds: the smooth-, the wirehaired, and the longhaired Dachshund, and, for example, Germany and

The three kinds of coats found on Dachshunds are shown here: short- or smooth-haired, wirehaired, and longhaired. But there are also differences in size and coat color.

France recognize the Kanninchen, the Dwarf, and the Standard.

There is also a great variety of colors with multiple combinations of black, tan, yellow, brown or gray, even white for the coat called Harlequin. In all, dozens of different dogs fall within this one breed!

Today, the Dachshund is first and foremost a companion dog, which does not mean that working stocks do not exist. It is simply necessary to be vigilant when purchasing one of these dogs. On the other hand, hunters often make the mistake of going directly toward wire-haired Dachshunds, while there are very good working stocks among short- and longhaired Dachshunds. In fact, in many European countries at the beginning of the 1990s, the most decorated Dachshund during field-trials was a black-and-tan longhaired Dachshund.

The training of this German dog demands great authority on the master's part because this dog's character is not always easy. Someone accustomed to hunting with pointers will be confounded by this dog's behavior.

However, with the development of flush hunting, the Dachshund can play an important role. With its small size it is particularly more useful for town-dwelling hunters. At its post, it can stay in the back-pack and come out only after the flushing of the game to go check whether the hunter's shots have hit his prey. Thus, this dog is often used when greater caution must be exercised in approaching game.

Field Trials

Of German origin, the Dachshund was developed to participate in numerous field trials that are also characteristically German. Fans of hounds would have difficulty figuring out what goes on in these field trials! Indeed, in various European countries there are no fewer than eleven different trials each of which is designated by acronyms for one or several German terms. These trials are divided into two large categories:

• Ground trials:

Sp: directed hare hunting

Sp/k: directed hunting on a released hare.

ST: training and quartering in woods.

SchwhK: blood tracking on a 24-hour old artificial trail.

Schwhk 40: blood tracking on a 40-hour old artificial trail.

SchwhKN: tracking on an artificial-natural trail.

VP: multiple trial that includes Sp, ST, and SchwhK.

• Underground trials:

BhFK: artificial foxhole trial.

BhFN: natural foxhole trial.

BhDN: natural badger-hole trial.

KschlH and ksPN: artificial or natural rabbit-hole trial reserved for Dwarf Dachshunds and Kanninchan.

Used in packs, the Dachshund is a formidable dog for big-game battue hunting. It gently pushes the animals toward the line, but also knows how to show determination when faced with recalcitrant wild boars.

Terriers

Terriers: Versatile Specialists

There are numerous breeds of terriers, almost all of them originally from Great Britain. These dogs were used mostly for fox hunting. Before they appeared, when an animal took shelter in a burrow, the hunt would come to a halt because the dogs were unable to drive the game from its hole. Then, the idea came to hunters that they should use dogs fit for going down underground tunnels, to force the animal out and thereby enable the hunt to go on. Later, terriers were used to eliminate harmful animals around farms and houses as well. Today, these dogs hunt both

underground and above ground. They hunt vermin underground and big game above ground.

Among all these breeds of terriers, only three are regularly used for hunting. All of the other breeds gave rise to companion dogs.

The Fox Terrier

Watch out! The Fox Terrier might be compared to dynamite. Always on the look-out, unable to sit still, it is constantly looking for ways to appease its over-flowing energy. Many town dwellers, taken in by its playfulness, later discovered the cruel truth: having a Fox

Terrier as a companion dog is not all fun and games!

On the other hand, it shows great effectiveness while hunting. Created in England for fox hunting, this dog later arrived in Continental Europe to hunt badgers and foxes underground. It did the hard work of digging. More recently, it met with considerable success with hunters who flushed wild boars.

Thus, the Fox Terrier is as courageous when game charges as when game stands at bay. With its baiting, it is able to draw the most recalcitrant wild boar out of its lair. Thanks to this new use, the numbers of Fox Terriers are on the rise today. However, one must be careful when purchasing these dogs, because

Previous page: Among the general public, the most well-known Fox Terrier is the Wirehaired Fox Terrier. But there is also a variety with short hair. Both of them are excellent for hunting in burrows as well as in thornbushes.

Below: Around the world many Fox Terriers are not used for hunting. Therefore, breeds must be chosen carefully to be sure that the puppies purchased were born of hunting parents.

many breeders still favor aesthetic criteria at the expense of working qualities.

There are two varieties of Fox Terrier: shorthaired and wirehaired.

The Jagd Terrier

Some dogs are cute, touching, or elegant. The Jagd Terrier is nothing of the kind! It is a killer. You must be a hunter to own several of these dogs or even just one. Underground, it shows exceptional courage, going down the burrow by itself to slay a few foxes or badgers. Its great valor, combined with an impressive aggressiveness, have recently made it successful with battue hunters of wild boars.

However, Germans originally wanted the Jagd to be more versatile. There, the Jagd Terrier must kill and retrieve harmful animals, fetch a wounded animal, or swim to fetch a winged duck.

It is difficult to make this dog live with other breeds, even with its own siblings. Fights are frequent and the owner must be very firm to control this dog.

The Jack Russell Terrier

The Jack Russell Terrier takes its name from a British pastor who, in the nineteenth century, decided to develop a terrier with a small frame that would be able to drive foxes out of the most narrow burrows during the famous fox hunts. Gaining official recognition in many countries as a breed less than ten years ago, it is very widespread as a companion dog in England where its "look" of caretaker dog is a big hit.

In France, for example, its presence is very recent. The very recently formed club of this breed tries to maintain its

Nowadays, the Jagd Terrier is very popular with wild boar hunters. This German Terrier is even more vicious with the black beast than the Fox Terrier is.

identity as a hunting dog more or less successfully. It is true that underground, it is fearless with foxes. Not used very much above ground, it is an excellent hunter of rabbits and it should attract wild boar hunters. However, its presence is too recent to expect the breed to develop very quickly.

As with the Fox Terrier, there is a variety with short hair and one with wiry hair.

The Jack Russell Terrier can also make an excellent watchdog. Able to participate in flushing big game as well as in cornering any kind of prey, it is the ideal companion for the professional gamekeeper's morning rounds on privately owned hunting grounds. One must keep in mind, however, that this dog has a true terrier temperament; some individuals are high strung.

Recently, the Jack Russell Terrier made a noticeable appearance in Europe. Despite the efforts of the Jack Russell Terrier Club, it is most commonly used as a companion dog.

Useful Addresses and Literature

KENNEL CLUBS

For General Information:

■ AMERICAN KENNEL CLUB
51 Madison Avenue
New York, New York, 10038
212-696-8200

For registration, records, or
litter information:
5580 Centerview Drive
Raleigh, NC 27606

■ AUSTRALIAN NATIONAL KENNEL CLUB
Royal Show Frounds
Ascot Vale
Victoria

■ CANADIAN KENNEL CLUB
111 Eglington Avenue
Toronto 12, Ontario

■ IRISH KENNEL CLUB
41 Harcourt Street
Dublin 2

■ THE KENNEL CLUB (GREAT BRITAIN)
1-4 Clargis Street
Picadilly
London, W7Y 8AB

■ NEW ZEALAND KENNEL CLUB
P.O. Box 523
Wellington

PUBLICATIONS

American Field
American Field Publishing
  Company
222 West Adams Street
Chicago, IL 60606
(Journal dating from 1874;
  covers all sporting breeds)

Hunter's Whistle, The ·
American Kennel Club
51 Madison Avenue
New York, New York 10038
(Bi-monthly newsletter;
  provides information on
  upcoming field trials and
  hunting tests.)

Retriever Field Trial News
4213 South Howell Avenue
Milwaukee, WI 53207
(Joint publication of the
  National Amateur Retriever
  Club and the National
  Retriever Club; compiles
  field trial statistics and covers
  news of the sport in the
  United States and Canada.)

BOOKS

Alderton, David, *The Dog Care Manual*, Barron's
  Educational Series, Inc.,
  Hauppauge, NY, 1986.
Baer, Ted, *Communicating with Your Dog*, Barron's
  Educational Series, Inc.,
  Hauppauge, NY, 1989.
S. Bulanda, *Boston Terriers*,
  Barron's Educational Series,
  Inc., Hauppauge, NY, 1994.
Carlson, Delbert, G., D.V.M.,
  and Griffin, James M., M.D.,
  Dog Owner's Home Veterinary Handbook,
  Howell Book House, New
  York, 1980.

Coile, D.C., *Jack Russell Terriers*, Barron's
  Educational Series, Inc.,
  Hauppauge, NY, 1996.
Ditto, T., *English Springer Spaniels*, Barron's
  Educational Series, Inc.,
  Hauppauge, NY, 1994.
Fiedelmeier, J., *Dachshunds*,
  Barron's Educational Series,
  Inc., Hauppauge, NY, 1994.
Fogle, Bruce, D.V.M.,
  M.R.C.V.S., *The Dog's Mind: Understanding Your Dog's Behavior*, Howell Book
  House, New York, 1990.
Kern, K., *Labrador Retrievers*,
  Barron's Educational Series,
  Inc., Hauppauge, NY, 1995.
Klever, U., *The Complete Book of Dog Care*, Barron's
  Educational Series, Inc.,
  Hauppauge, NY, 1989.
Kriechbanner, A., *Yorkshire Terriers*, Barron's
  Educational Series, Inc.,
  Hauppauge, NY, 1990.
Parent, L., *Beagles*, Barron's
  Educational Series, Inc.,
  Hauppauge, NY, 1995.
Rice, D., *The Complete Book of Dog Breeding*, Barron's
  Educational Series, Inc.,
  Hauppauge, NY, 1996.
Schneidermann, B., *Retrievers*,
  Barron's Educational Series,
  Inc., Hauppauge, NY, 1996.
Stahlkuppe, J., *Irish Setters*,
  Barron's Educational Series,
  Inc., Hauppauge, NY, 1992.
Sucher, J., *Golden Retrievers*,
  Barron's Educational Series,
  Inc., Hauppauge, NY, 1995.
Ullmann, H. J. and E.,
  Spaniels, Barron's
  Educational Series, Inc.,
  Hauppauge, NY, 1982.

If you want to know more about French dog breeds, please contact the following breed associations which are all affiliated with the Central Canine Society.

■ SOCIÉTÉ CENTRALE CANINE
[CENTRAL CANINE SOCIETY]
155, avenue Jean-Jaurès
95535 Aubervilliers Cedex
FRANCE
Tel.: 33.1.49.37.54.00

■ CLUB FRANÇAIS DES TERRIERS DIVERS
(DONT LE JACK RUSSEL TERRIER) [FRENCH TERRIERS CLUB (INCLUDING THE JACK RUSSELL TERRIER)]
M. Parson
5, avenue du Verseau
44700 Orvault
FRANCE
Tel.: 33.40.40.59.15
Fax: 33.40.76.79.91

■ RÉUNION DES AMATEURS DE FOX-TERRIERS
[ASSOCIATION OF FOX-TERRIER LOVERS]
Mme Pelissier
La Fontaine-en-Gemages
61130 Bellème
FRANCE
Hours: Secretary
Mondays, Wednesdays and
Fridays, 9:00–12:30, 2:30–6:00
Tel.: 33.33.83.31.37
Fax: 33.33.83.73.72
Tuesdays, 2:00–6:30
Tel.: 33.68.60.45.69

■ JAGD-TERRIER CLUB DE FRANCE [JAGD TERRIER CLUB OF FRANCE]
M. Alvaro Marson
17, impasse des Artisans
74460 Marnaz
FRANCE
Tel.: 33.50.98.92

Hounds and Bloodhounds

■ CLUB FRANÇAIS DU CHIEN DE SAINT-HUBERT (FRENCH SAINT HUBERT CLUB) (in the process of formation)
M. Jean-Pierre Boitard
La Chesnaie
Route de la Forge
27250 Rugles
FRANCE
Tel.: 33.32.24.69.95

■ CLUB DU CHIEN D'ORDRE [DOGS OF RANK CLUB]
M. Pierre Astié
Logis de la Grange
86240 Fontaine-le-Comte
FRANCE
Tel.: 33.49.57.04.45

■ CLUB DU GRIFFON VENDÉEN [GRIFFON FROM THE VENDÉE CLUB]
M. Renaud Buche
Chemin de l'Ermitage
27930 Huest
FRANCE
Tel.: 33.32.34.18.62

■ CLUB DU BASSET ARTÉSIEN NORMAND ET DU CHIEN D'ARTOIS [CLUB OF THE ARTESIEN BASSET HOUND OF NORMANDY AND THE ARTOIS HOUND]
M. Maurice Leblanc
45210 La Selle-sur-le-Bied
FRANCE
Tel.: 33.38.87.30.03

■ CLUB DE L'ANGLO-FRANÇAIS DE PETITE VÉNERIE [THE ANGLO-FRENCH OF SMALL-GAME HUNTING CLUB]
M. Jean-Paul Rogeon
3, avenue de la Gare
79201 Parthenay Cedex
FRANCE
Tel.: 33.49.64.05.02
Fax: 33.49.94.01.64

■ CLUB DU BLEU DE GASCOGNE, GASCON SAINTONGEOIS ET ARIÉGEOIS [CLUB OF GASCONY, AND ARIÉGEOIS HOUNDS]
M. Gérard Thonnat
Avenue de la Bageasse
43100 Brioude
FRANCE
Tel.: 33.71.74.92.27

■ CLUB DU PORCELAINE [PORCELAIN CLUB]
M. Jean-Pierre Michel
Parc de la Romane
La Machotte
84190 Gigondas
FRANCE
Tel.: 33.90.65.87.39

■ CLUB DE FAUVE DE BRETAGNE [FAWN-COLORED BRITTANY CLUB]
M. Dominique Ryckebusch
Le Renclos de Bussac
17550 Dolus d'Oléron
FRANCE
Tel.: 33.46.75.36.40

■ CLUB DU GRIFFON NIVERNAIS [NIVERNAIS GRIFFON CLUB]
M. Kohler
7, rue G.-Chaumette
58000 Nevers
FRANCE

■ CLUB DU BRUNO DU JURA ET CHIENS COURANTS SUISSES [BRUNO JURA HOUND AND SWISS HOUND CLUB]
M. Patrick Guénolé
Le Goascaer
29228 Plougasnou
FRANCE
Tel.: 33.98.72.32.87
Fax: 33.98.72.41.56

■ CLUB FRANÇAIS DU CHIEN DE ROUGE DU HANOVRE ET DE BAVIÈRE [THE FRENCH CLUB OF THE HANOVER AND BAVARIAN BLOODHOUND] (in the process of formation)
M. Gilbert Titeux
11, place du Waldacker
Osenbach
68570 Soulzmatt
FRANCE
Tel.: 33.89.47.06.50

Pointers

■ CLUB FRANÇAIS DU BRAQUE ALLEMAND [THE FRENCH CLUB OF THE GERMAN HOUND]
M. Jean-Claude Bernard
150, avenue Parmentier
75011 Paris
FRANCE
Tel.: 33.1.48.05.80.57

■ DRAHTHAAR CLUB DE FRANCE [DRAHTHAAR CLUB OF FRANCE]
M. Maurice Lecoint
11, rue du Puits-d'Argent
02240 Itancourt
FRANCE
Tel.: 33.23.08.70.22
    or 33.23.08.67.18
Fax: 33.23.68.62.59

■ CERCLE DES AMATEURS DU BRAQUE DE WEIMAR [WEIMAR HOUND LOVERS CIRCLE]
M. Michel Pelletier
134, le Petit Cossole-Les Chapelles
45520 Chevilly
FRANCE
Tel.: 33.38.74.15.71

■ RÉUNION DES AMATEURS DU BRAQUE D'AUVERGNE [AUVERGNE HOUND LOVERS GROUP]
M. Lassandre
Peyzat
23380 Glénic
FRANCE
Tel.: 33.55.81.89.89

■ CLUB DU BRAQUE DU BOURBONNAIS [BOURBON HOUND CLUB]
M. Pierre-Marc Tixier
Toury-sur-Jour
58240 Saint-Pierre-le-Moutier
FRANCE
Tel.: 33.86.98.61.02

■ CLUB DU BRAQUE FRANÇAIS (ET CLUB DU BRAQUE DE L'ARIÈGE) [FRENCH HOUND CLUB (AND ARIÈGE HOUND CLUB)]
Mme Ceriana
Pin vert, Clos Mireille
Allée J.-Aicard
13400 Aubagne
FRANCE
Tel.: 33.42.03.11.99
Fax: 33.42.03.48.03

■ CLUB DU BRAQUE SAINT-GERMAIN [SAINT GERMAIN HOUND CLUB]
Mme Denise Clergeau
La Sauzaie – Saint-Xandré
17138 Puilboreau
FRANCE
Tel.: 33.46.37.30.96

■ CLUB FRANÇAIS DU BRAQUE HONGROIS – VISZLA CLUB DE FRANCE (ET SPINONE ET BRAQUE ITALIEN) [FRENCH HUNGARIAN HOUND CLUB - VISZLA CLUB OF FRANCE (AND SPINONE AND ITALIAN HOUND)]
Mme Natalie Parent
11, rue Jules-Ferry
59127 Walincourt
FRANCE
Tel.: 33.27.78.83.83
Fax: 33.27.82.74.73

■ CLUB FRANÇAIS DE L'ÉPAGNEUL DE MÜNSTER ET DU LANGHAAR [FRENCH CLUB OF THE MÜNSTER SPANIEL AND THE LANGHAAR]
M. Antony Andrieu
1560, route de Caromb
84380 Mazan
FRANCE
Tel.: 33.90.69.63.67

■ CLUB DE L'ÉPAGNEUL
PICARD, DU BLEU DE
PICARDIE ET DE L'ÉPAGNEUL
DE PONT-AUDEMER [PICARDY
SPANIEL, BLUE PICARDY
SPANIEL AND PONT-AUDEMER
SPANIEL CLUB]
M. Philippe Régnier
Le Bec Etoilé
80620 Domart-en-Ponthieu
FRANCE

■ CLUB DE L'ÉPAGNEUL
BRETON [BRITTANY SPANIEL
CLUB]
M. Léon Le Louet
D. 833
27220 Mousseaux-Neuville
FRANCE

■ CLUB DE L'ÉPAGNEUL
FRANÇAIS [FRENCH SPANIEL
CLUB]
M. Henry Loraux
B.P. 29
74330 La Balme-de-Sillingy
FRANCE
Tel.: 33.50.68.89.05

■ CLUB DU GRIFFON D'ARRÊT
À POIL DUR KORTHALS [WIRE-
HAIRED POINTER KORTHALS
GRIFFON CLUB]
M. Jacques Carpentier
Le Ruisseau du Massacre
Gaillard-Tournie
31190 Grépiac
FRANCE

■ RED CLUB
[BLOODHOUND CLUB]
Mme Claudine Poillong
3, rue Rémont
78000 Versailles
FRANCE
Tel.: 33.1.39.53.13.71

■ RÉUNION DES AMATEURS
DE SETTERS GORDON
[GORDON SETTER LOVERS
GROUP]
M. Barnili
30, rue du Chevalleret
45510 Tigy
FRANCE
Tel.: 33.38.58.01.61

Flushing Dogs and Water Dogs

■ SPANIEL CLUB FRANÇAIS
[FRENCH SPANIEL CLUB]
Mme Fabienne Courtel
Les Bruyères
Avesnes-en-Bray
76220 Gournay-en-Bray
FRANCE
Tel.: 35.33.90.04.60

■ CLUB DES CHIENS D'EAU
[WATER DOGS CLUB]
M. Jean-Claude Hermans
11, avenue de Tobrouk
78500 Sartrouville
FRANCE
Tel.: 33.1.39.68.86.88
Fax: 33.1.39.81.18.12
or Mme Josée Guinard
21, rue de Corbeil-Cerf
Le Déluge
60790 Valdampierre
FRANCE
Tel.: 33.44.79.21.11

Correspondant Member

■ SOCIÉTÉ DE VÉNERIE
[HUNTING SOCIETY]
M. Diego de Bodard
10, rue de Lisbonne
75008 Paris
FRANCE
Secretary, same address
Tel.: 33.1.42.93.24.31

ASSOCIATION OF PROFESSIONAL TRAINERS OF POINTERS, RETRIEVERS, AND FLUSHING DOGS

Le Paré
77120 Chailly-en-Brie
FRANCE
Tel.: 33.1.64.04.61.76
Fax: 33.1.64.04.69.24

Index

A

Age considerations, 23–25
Aggression, 40
American Field, 216
American Kennel Club, 216
Anglo-French Hound, 188
Ariege Beagle, 183
Artesian Basset of Normandy, 178–179
Artois Dog, 187
Australian National Kennel Club, 216
Auvergne Hound, 108

B

Barking, 60
Basset:
    Artesian of Normandy, 178–179
    Blue Gascony, 181
    Fawn Brittany, 179–180
    Hound, 198
    Large, 186
    Petit, Griffon Vendeen, 180–181
Beagle, 186, 197–198
    Anglo-French Hound, 188
    Ariege, 183
    Artois, 187
    Blue Gascony Griffon, 184
    Fawn Brittany Griffon, 185–186
    French, 182–189
    Griffon from the Vendée Region, 186
    Harrier, 188–189
    Little Saintonge Gascony, 185–186
    Nevers Griffon, 187–188
    Porcelain, 186–187
    Small Blue Gascony, 183
Bedding, 29
Behavior, 39–45
Billy, 191–194
Bloodhounds, 64–65, 80–81, 202–203
    field trials, 80–81
    training, 64–65
Blue Gascony:
    Basset, 181
    Griffon, 184
Blue Picardy Spaniel, 95, 103–104
Bourbon Hound, 108–109
Breed, selection, 18–20

B (continued)

British:
    hounds, 196–199
    pointers, 113–123
Brittany Spaniel, 97–102
Bruno Jura Hound, 200–201

C

Canadian Kennel Club, 216
Chesapeake Bay Retriever, 149–150
Clumber Spaniel, 165
Cocker spaniel, 160–162
Collars, electronic, 51
Commands, 36, 38
Competition, 70
    See also: Field Trials, Shows
Continental Water Dogs, 155
Crossbreeds, 22
Curly-Coated Retriever, 148–149

D

Dachshunds, 206–209
    field trials, 209
Dietary supplements, 33
Distemper, 31
Domination, 41
"Down" command, 51–52
Drahtaar, 128–130

E

Electronic collars, 51
English:
    Setter, 118–120
    Springer Spaniel, 162–164

F

Fawn Brittany:
    Basset, 179–180
    Griffon, 185–186
Feeding, 32–33
Field:
    Spaniel, 165–166

Table of Contents